SBA 504 Mortgage Loans for Commercial Real Estate

Long-Term Fixed-Rate SBA Mortgage Financing for Large Property Purchases

By Joseph G. Correa

Licensed Mortgage Broker, Finibi Mortgage

Copyright & Legal Notice

Published by Live Stronger Faster

The information provided in this book is for educational and informational purposes only and does not constitute financial, legal, tax, or investment advice. Although the author is a licensed mortgage professional, the content presented is general in nature and is not intended as personalized guidance for any specific individual, business, or financial situation.

The strategies, loan structures, and examples discussed in this book are illustrative and educational in nature. They are intended to demonstrate concepts related to SBA commercial mortgage financing, including SBA 7(a) and 504 loan programs, borrower qualification, debt service coverage analysis, property acquisition, refinancing, construction financing, and advanced loan structuring. These examples do not represent guaranteed approvals, loan terms, or outcomes. Results may vary significantly based on individual financial profiles, credit history, business performance, property type, market conditions, and lender-specific guidelines.

SBA loan programs are subject to eligibility requirements, regulatory guidelines, and changes established by the U.S. Small Business Administration and participating lenders. Borrowers are encouraged to consult directly with qualified financial, legal, and tax professionals before making any financing or investment decisions.

The author and publisher make no representations or warranties regarding the accuracy, completeness, or applicability of the content and disclaim any liability for errors, omissions, or outcomes resulting from the use or misuse of the information contained in this book.

First Edition, 2026

Table of Contents

Introduction

In the world of commercial real estate financing, few tools are as powerful, misunderstood, and underutilized as the SBA 504 mortgage loan. While many investors and business owners are familiar with traditional bank loans or even SBA 7(a) financing, the SBA 504 program stands in a category of its own—designed specifically to provide long-term, fixed-rate financing for large commercial real estate purchases and capital-intensive projects. This book, *SBA 504 Mortgage Loans for Commercial Real Estate*, is your complete guide to understanding, structuring, and leveraging this unique financing vehicle to build long-term wealth, stability, and control over your business operations.

The SBA 504 loan is not just a loan—it is a strategic financial instrument. It allows business owners to acquire, build, or refinance owner-occupied commercial real estate with lower down payments, below-market fixed interest rates, and extended repayment terms that can reach up to 25 years. Unlike many conventional loans that expose borrowers to interest rate risk or require significant equity upfront, the SBA 504 program is built to support growth, encourage economic development, and provide stability in an otherwise volatile financing environment. This means that when used correctly, it can become a cornerstone of a long-term real estate and business expansion strategy.

At its core, the SBA 504 loan is structured differently from most traditional loans. It typically involves three parties: a conventional lender, a Certified Development Company (CDC), and the borrower. The bank provides a portion of the financing, usually around 50 percent of the total project cost. The CDC, backed by the Small Business Administration, provides up to 40 percent through a debenture that carries a fixed interest rate. The borrower typically contributes as little as 10 percent down, although this can vary depending on the project type, property use, and borrower experience. This layered structure creates a powerful leverage opportunity, allowing borrowers to control large, income-producing assets with relatively minimal upfront capital.

One of the most compelling features of the SBA 504 program is its long-term, fixed-rate component. In a market where interest rates can fluctuate significantly, locking in a fixed rate for 20 to 25 years provides predictability and peace of mind. For business owners, this translates into stable monthly payments, easier budgeting, and protection against rising interest rates. Over time, this stability can significantly enhance cash flow management and improve the overall financial health of the business. It also allows entrepreneurs to focus on growth, operations, and profitability rather than constantly worrying about refinancing or rate adjustments.

Another key advantage of SBA 504 loans is their focus on owner-occupied commercial real estate. This requirement aligns perfectly with business owners who want to transition from leasing to owning their operating space. Instead of paying rent to a landlord and building someone else's equity, borrowers can use SBA 504 financing to acquire their own property, build equity over time, and potentially benefit from property appreciation. This shift from tenant to owner is often a transformative step in a business owner's journey, providing not only financial benefits but also greater control over the business environment.

Throughout this book, you will learn how to identify the best opportunities for SBA 504 financing and how to structure deals that meet both SBA guidelines and lender expectations. You will gain a deep understanding of eligibility requirements, including occupancy rules, business qualifications, and property types. You will also learn how to navigate the application process, from initial prequalification to final loan approval and closing. Each step will be broken down into clear, actionable strategies that you can apply immediately, whether you are a first-time borrower or an experienced investor looking to expand your portfolio. In addition to the fundamentals, this book will dive into advanced strategies for maximizing the benefits of SBA 504 loans. You will discover how to combine SBA 504 financing with other capital sources, how to structure deals to minimize your down payment, and how to position your business to qualify for the most favorable terms. You will also learn how to evaluate different project types, including acquisitions, ground-up construction, and major renovations, and determine which scenarios are best suited for SBA 504 financing.

A critical aspect of mastering SBA 504 loans is understanding the long-term implications of your financing decisions. This includes analyzing cash flow, projecting future growth, and planning for eventual exit strategies. Unlike short-term financing options, SBA 504 loans are designed to support long-term ownership and stability. This means that every decision you make—from property selection to loan structuring—should be aligned with your long-term business and investment goals. This book will guide you through that process, helping you think strategically and make decisions that position you for sustained success.

You will also explore the role of economic development in SBA 504 lending. The program is designed not only to benefit individual borrowers but also to stimulate job creation and economic growth within communities. As a borrower, your project may qualify for additional benefits or incentives based on its impact on local employment and development. Understanding these factors can give you a competitive advantage and open the door to more favorable financing terms.

As you progress through this book, you will notice a recurring theme: leverage with control. The SBA 504 loan allows you to leverage capital efficiently while maintaining control over your business and real estate. This combination is rare in the world of commercial financing and is one of the primary reasons why sophisticated investors and business owners rely on this program to scale their operations. By mastering the concepts and strategies outlined in this book, you will be equipped to use SBA 504 loans not just as a financing tool, but as a long-term wealth-building mechanism.

This book is designed to be both educational and practical. It does not assume prior experience with SBA loans or commercial real estate, but it also goes deep enough to provide value to seasoned professionals. Whether you are looking to purchase your first commercial property, expand your existing business, or build a diversified real estate portfolio, the strategies in this book will help you achieve your goals more efficiently and with greater confidence.

By the end of this journey, you will have a clear understanding of how SBA 504 mortgage loans work, when to use them, and how to structure deals that maximize their benefits. You will be able to identify opportunities that others overlook, avoid common pitfalls that can derail approvals, and position yourself as a knowledgeable and strategic borrower in the eyes of lenders and partners.

The path to building wealth through commercial real estate is not reserved for large corporations or institutional investors. With the right knowledge, strategy, and execution, it is accessible to any motivated entrepreneur or business owner. The SBA 504 loan is one of the most powerful tools available to help you achieve that vision. This book will show you how to use it effectively, strategically, and confidently, so you can take control of your financial future and build a lasting legacy through commercial real estate ownership.

Chapter 1

Understanding the SBA 504 Mortgage Loan Structure and Why It Is Powerful for Commercial Real Estate

The SBA 504 mortgage loan is one of the most powerful yet misunderstood tools available for commercial real estate financing, and mastering its structure is the first step toward using it effectively to build long-term wealth. At a surface level, it may appear similar to other loan programs, but once you begin to break down how it is designed, you quickly realize that it offers advantages that traditional financing simply cannot match. This chapter is dedicated to helping you fully understand how the SBA 504 loan works, why it was created, and how its structure gives you a strategic edge as a borrower, business owner, and investor.

The SBA 504 loan was created to support economic development by helping small businesses acquire fixed assets such as commercial real estate and large equipment. Unlike many financing options that prioritize lender flexibility or short-term gains, the SBA 504 program is designed with long-term stability in mind. The goal is to allow business owners to secure permanent financing that supports growth without exposing them to unnecessary financial risk. This is especially important in commercial real estate, where large capital investments and long holding periods require predictable and stable financing structures.

What makes the SBA 504 loan unique is its three-party structure. Instead of relying on a single lender to fund the entire project, the financing is split into two primary components: a conventional lender portion and a CDC portion. The conventional lender, typically a bank or credit union, provides approximately 50 percent of the total project cost. The CDC, which is a nonprofit organization certified by the Small Business Administration, provides up to 40 percent of the financing through a debenture backed by the SBA. The borrower then contributes the remaining portion, usually around 10 percent, although this can increase depending on factors such as the type of property, whether the business is considered a startup, or if the property is deemed special-purpose.

This structure is powerful because it reduces risk for all parties involved while maximizing leverage for the borrower. The bank benefits from having a lower loan-to-value position, which reduces its exposure. The CDC provides long-term, fixed-rate financing that enhances the stability of the overall loan. And the borrower gains access to a financing structure that requires less upfront capital than traditional commercial loans, which often require 20 to 30 percent down. This means that with the SBA 504 program, you can control a significantly larger asset with less cash, freeing up capital for other investments or operational needs.

Another defining feature of the SBA 504 loan is the fixed interest rate associated with the CDC portion of the loan. This fixed-rate component typically spans 20 to 25 years, providing a level of predictability that is rarely available in commercial real estate financing. In contrast, many conventional loans offer variable rates or shorter fixed-rate periods that eventually adjust, exposing borrowers to interest rate risk. With the SBA 504 structure, a substantial portion of your loan remains fixed for decades, allowing you to plan your finances with confidence and avoid the uncertainty that comes with fluctuating rates.

The importance of this fixed-rate stability cannot be overstated. Over time, even small increases in interest rates can significantly impact your monthly payments and overall cash flow. By locking in a fixed rate for a large portion of your financing, you effectively hedge against future rate increases. This can be especially valuable in environments where interest rates are expected to rise or remain volatile. For business owners, stable payments translate into better budgeting, improved financial planning, and the ability to reinvest profits into growth rather than covering unexpected increases in debt service.

One of the key eligibility requirements of the SBA 504 loan is that the property must be owner-occupied. This means that your business must occupy at least 51 percent of an existing building or 60 percent of a newly constructed property, with plans to occupy more over time. While this requirement may initially seem limiting, it actually aligns perfectly with the goals of many business owners. Instead of leasing space and building equity for a landlord, you are investing in your own property and creating a long-term asset that can appreciate in value and provide additional income opportunities.

Owning your business property also provides a level of control that leasing simply cannot offer. You are no longer subject to lease renewals, rent increases, or restrictions imposed by landlords. You can customize the space to meet your operational needs, expand as your business grows, and potentially lease out unused portions of the property to generate additional income. This combination of operational control and financial benefit is one of the primary reasons why many successful entrepreneurs prioritize property ownership as part of their long-term strategy. Another important aspect of the SBA 504 loan is its focus on job creation and economic impact. The program is designed to support projects that contribute to local economic development, which often includes creating or retaining jobs. While this requirement can vary depending on the specific project and industry, it is an important consideration when structuring your deal. By aligning your project with these goals, you may be able to access additional benefits or improve your chances of approval.

As you begin to understand the SBA 504 loan, it is essential to recognize that it is not just about financing—it is about strategy. The way you structure your loan, select your property, and position your business can have a significant impact on your long-term success. This means that every decision you make should be intentional and aligned with your overall goals. Whether you are acquiring your first commercial property or expanding an existing portfolio, the SBA 504 loan provides a framework that supports growth, stability, and wealth creation.

In the chapters that follow, you will dive deeper into each component of the SBA 504 loan, including eligibility requirements, application processes, underwriting criteria, and advanced structuring techniques. You will learn how to identify opportunities, avoid common pitfalls, and position yourself as a strong borrower in the eyes of lenders and CDCs.

By building a solid foundation of knowledge in this chapter, you are preparing yourself to take full advantage of one of the most powerful financing tools available in commercial real estate.

Ultimately, the SBA 504 loan is more than just a way to finance property—it is a pathway to ownership, control, and long-term financial independence. By understanding its structure and leveraging its advantages, you can transform the way you approach commercial real estate and position yourself for sustained success in an increasingly competitive market.

Real-Life Math Example: Structuring an SBA 504 Loan for a Commercial Property Purchase

To fully understand the power of the SBA 504 loan, it is essential to walk through a detailed real-life example that illustrates how the numbers work and how this financing structure can transform a deal. In this example, we will follow a business owner named Maria, who is looking to purchase a commercial property for her growing logistics company. Maria has been leasing warehouse space for several years, but rising rent and limited control over the property have motivated her to explore ownership.

Maria identifies a property priced at $2,000,000 that perfectly suits her operational needs. The building is located in a strategic area, has sufficient square footage for her current operations, and includes additional space that she can lease to other tenants for supplemental income. Instead of pursuing a traditional commercial loan, which would require a 25 percent down payment of $500,000, Maria decides to explore an SBA 504 loan to reduce her upfront capital requirement.

Using the SBA 504 structure, the financing is divided into three components. The conventional lender agrees to provide 50 percent of the total project cost, which amounts to $1,000,000. The CDC provides 40 percent, which equals $800,000, through a fixed-rate debenture. Maria is responsible for the remaining 10 percent, which is $200,000. Immediately, you can see the advantage: instead of needing $500,000 for a traditional loan, Maria only needs $200,000, allowing her to preserve $300,000 in capital that she can use for business expansion, equipment purchases, or working capital.

Now let's break down the monthly payments to understand how this structure impacts cash flow. The bank portion of $1,000,000 is financed at an interest rate of 6.5 percent with a 25-year amortization. This results in a monthly payment of approximately $6,750. The CDC portion of $800,000 is financed at a fixed rate of 5.5 percent over 25 years, resulting in a monthly payment of approximately $4,900. When combined, Maria's total monthly debt service is approximately $11,650.

Next, we compare this to her previous leasing situation. Maria was paying $14,000 per month in rent, with annual increases built into her lease agreement. By purchasing the property using an SBA 504 loan, she not only reduces her monthly occupancy cost by over $2,000 but also begins building equity in a valuable commercial asset. Over time, as rents in the area increase and her loan balance decreases, her financial position strengthens significantly.

In addition to the cost savings, Maria also generates additional income by leasing out a portion of the property. She rents out 30 percent of the building to another business for $4,000 per month. This rental income effectively reduces her net occupancy cost to $7,650 per month, creating a powerful cash flow advantage compared to her previous lease.

Over a 10-year period, the benefits become even more pronounced. Maria's loan balance decreases as she makes payments, while the property appreciates in value. If the property increases in value by just 3 percent annually, it would be worth approximately $2,687,000 after 10 years. At the same time, her loan balance would have been significantly reduced, creating substantial equity that she can leverage for future investments or business expansion.

This example highlights the true power of the SBA 504 loan: it allows you to acquire a high-value asset with minimal upfront capital, reduce your monthly costs, generate additional income, and build long-term wealth through appreciation and equity growth. By understanding how to structure these deals and analyze the numbers, you can make informed decisions that align with your financial goals and set yourself up for long-term success.

As you continue through this book, you will encounter more advanced examples and strategies that build on this foundation. Each scenario will provide deeper insights into how to maximize the benefits of SBA 504 financing and apply these concepts to real-world opportunities. The key is to not only understand the numbers but to use them strategically to create opportunities that others may overlook.

Chapter 2

Eligibility Requirements, Property Types, and Borrower Qualifications for SBA 504 Mortgage Loans

Understanding the eligibility requirements for SBA 504 mortgage loans is one of the most critical steps in successfully structuring and closing a commercial real estate deal. While the SBA 504 program offers powerful advantages such as low down payments, long-term fixed rates, and favorable terms, it is also governed by specific guidelines that must be met by both the borrower and the property. These requirements are not obstacles; rather, they are a framework designed to ensure that the program supports stable, growth-oriented businesses that contribute to economic development. When you understand these guidelines deeply, you gain the ability to structure deals proactively, avoid delays, and significantly increase your chances of approval.

At the borrower level, the SBA 504 program is designed for for-profit businesses operating within the United States. This includes a wide range of entities such as corporations, limited liability companies, partnerships, and sole proprietorships. One of the most important qualifications is that the business must meet the SBA's definition of a small business. This is typically based on either net worth or net income thresholds, which are designed to ensure that the program supports businesses that genuinely need access to favorable financing. Generally, the business must have a tangible net worth of less than $15 million and an average net income of less than $5 million over the previous two years, although these figures can evolve with SBA updates.

In addition to meeting size standards, borrowers must demonstrate the ability to repay the loan. This involves a thorough review of financial statements, tax returns, and cash flow projections. Lenders and CDCs will analyze the business's historical performance as well as its future potential. They want to see consistent revenue, manageable expenses, and sufficient cash flow to cover the proposed debt service. This is often measured using a debt service coverage ratio, which compares the business's net operating income to its total debt obligations. A strong DSCR indicates that the business generates enough income to comfortably meet its loan payments, which is a key factor in securing approval.

Creditworthiness is another essential component of borrower eligibility. While SBA 504 loans are more flexible than many conventional financing options, lenders still expect borrowers to demonstrate responsible credit behavior. This includes a solid credit score, a history of on-time payments, and minimal derogatory events such as bankruptcies or foreclosures. However, it is important to note that the SBA 504 program is not exclusively reserved for perfect borrowers. In many cases, strong business performance and a well-structured deal can offset moderate credit challenges, especially when the overall risk profile remains acceptable.

Equity injection, or the borrower's down payment, is also a key requirement. In most cases, the borrower is expected to contribute at least 10 percent of the total project cost. However, this requirement can increase to 15 or even 20 percent depending on factors such as whether the business is a startup or if the property is considered special-purpose. Special-purpose properties are those that have limited alternative uses, such as hotels, gas stations, or medical facilities. Because these properties carry higher risk from a lender's perspective, they require a higher equity contribution to offset that risk.

One of the most defining eligibility criteria for SBA 504 loans is the owner-occupancy requirement. The property being financed must be primarily occupied by the borrower's business. For existing buildings, the business must occupy at least 51 percent of the space. For new construction, the initial occupancy requirement is 60 percent, with plans to increase occupancy over time. This requirement ensures that the program supports businesses that are actively using the property for their operations, rather than purely passive real estate investments.

While the owner-occupancy requirement limits the use of SBA 504 loans for fully leased investment properties, it still provides significant flexibility. Borrowers can lease out a portion of the property, as long as they meet the occupancy thresholds. This creates an opportunity to generate additional income while maintaining compliance with SBA guidelines. Over time, as the business grows, the borrower can expand into previously leased space, further increasing their control and utilization of the property.

The types of properties eligible for SBA 504 financing are generally those that are considered fixed assets. This includes office buildings, warehouses, manufacturing facilities, retail spaces, and certain specialized properties. The program can be used for purchasing existing buildings, constructing new facilities, or renovating and improving existing properties. It can also be used for large equipment purchases that have a long useful life. However, working capital, inventory, and speculative real estate investments are not eligible under the SBA 504 program. Another important aspect of eligibility is the concept of public policy goals. The SBA 504 program is designed to promote economic development, which often includes job creation or retention. In many cases, borrowers are expected to create or retain a certain number of jobs relative to the loan amount. However, there are alternative ways to meet these requirements, such as supporting community development, advancing green energy initiatives, or benefiting underserved markets. Understanding these options allows you to position your project in a way that aligns with SBA objectives and enhances your approval potential.

The borrower's experience and management capability also play a significant role in the approval process. Lenders and CDCs want to see that the borrower has the knowledge and expertise to successfully operate the business and manage the property. This includes industry experience, a track record of performance, and a clear business plan. If the borrower lacks direct experience, they may still qualify by demonstrating strong support systems, such as experienced management teams or industry advisors.

As you can see, eligibility for an SBA 504 loan is not based on a single factor, but rather a combination of financial strength, operational stability, and strategic alignment with SBA goals. The key is to approach the process with a comprehensive understanding of these requirements and to structure your deal in a way that meets or exceeds them. By doing so, you not only increase your chances of approval but also position yourself as a strong, credible borrower in the eyes of lenders and CDCs.

This chapter provides the foundation for everything that follows. By mastering these eligibility requirements, you will be able to identify viable opportunities, avoid common mistakes, and move through the loan process with confidence. In the next chapters, you will build on this knowledge by exploring the application process, underwriting criteria, and advanced structuring strategies that will take your SBA 504 expertise to the next level.

Real-Life Math Example: Evaluating Eligibility and Structuring a Qualified SBA 504 Deal

To fully understand how eligibility requirements translate into real-world decision-making, let's walk through a detailed example involving a borrower named David, who owns a growing manufacturing business. David is looking to purchase a commercial property to expand his operations and reduce his reliance on leased space. He identifies a property priced at $3,000,000 that includes a large warehouse, office space, and room for future expansion.

The first step is determining whether David's business qualifies as a small business under SBA guidelines. After reviewing his financial statements, we find that his business has a tangible net worth of $8,000,000 and an average net income of $2,500,000 over the past two years. These figures fall well within the SBA limits, making him eligible from a size perspective. Next, we evaluate his ability to repay the loan by analyzing his cash flow.

David's business generates annual net operating income of $600,000. Based on the proposed SBA 504 loan structure, the total loan amount would be $2,700,000, with David contributing a 10 percent down payment of $300,000. The bank provides $1,500,000 at 6.75 percent, and the CDC provides $1,200,000 at 5.75 percent. The combined annual debt service for both loans is approximately $215,000. When we divide David's net operating income of $600,000 by his annual debt service of $215,000, we get a debt service coverage ratio of approximately 2.79. This is a very strong DSCR, indicating that David's business generates nearly three times the income needed to cover the loan payments.

Next, we evaluate the occupancy requirement. David plans to use 70 percent of the building for his manufacturing operations and lease out the remaining 30 percent to a complementary business. This meets the SBA requirement for owner-occupied properties, as he exceeds the 51 percent threshold for existing buildings. The rental income from the leased portion is projected at $8,000 per month, or $96,000 annually, which further strengthens his financial position. Now let's examine the impact of this rental income on David's overall cash flow. His annual debt service is $215,000, but the rental income reduces his effective cost to $119,000. When we compare this to his previous leasing expenses of $180,000 per year, we see an immediate improvement in cash flow of $61,000 annually. This not only enhances profitability but also provides additional funds that can be reinvested into the business.

We also consider the long-term appreciation of the property. If the property increases in value at an average rate of 3 percent per year, it would be worth approximately $4,031,000 after 10 years. At the same time, David's loan balance would have decreased significantly due to principal payments. This combination of appreciation and loan amortization creates substantial equity, which David can leverage for future investments or expansions.

Finally, we evaluate the equity injection requirement. Because David's business is well-established and the property is not considered special-purpose, he qualifies for the standard 10 percent down payment. This allows him to conserve $600,000 compared to a traditional 30 percent down payment scenario, giving him additional liquidity to invest in equipment, hiring, or marketing.

This example demonstrates how understanding eligibility requirements and applying them strategically can transform a deal. By meeting SBA guidelines and structuring the financing effectively, David is able to acquire a high-value asset, improve his cash flow, generate additional income, and build long-term wealth. The key is not just understanding the numbers, but using them to create opportunities that align with both SBA objectives and your personal financial goals.

Chapter 3

The SBA 504 Loan Process from Prequalification to Closing

Understanding how the SBA 504 loan works conceptually is important, but knowing how to actually navigate the process from start to finish is what separates successful borrowers from those who get stuck, delayed, or denied. The SBA 504 loan process is structured, detailed, and documentation-heavy, but when approached correctly, it becomes predictable and manageable. This chapter will walk you step-by-step through the full lifecycle of an SBA 504 loan—from the moment you identify a property to the day you close and take ownership—so you can move through the process with confidence and control.

The process begins with prequalification, which is often overlooked but critically important. At this stage, you are not yet applying for the loan formally. Instead, you are working with a lender or CDC to determine whether you are a strong candidate for SBA 504 financing. This involves reviewing your business financials, personal financials, credit profile, and overall deal structure. The goal of prequalification is to identify any potential issues early and address them before they become obstacles. A strong prequalification can also give you leverage when negotiating with sellers, as it demonstrates that you are a serious and capable buyer.

Once prequalified, the next step is identifying and securing the property. This involves negotiating a purchase agreement that is contingent on financing approval. It is essential to include sufficient time for the SBA loan process, which can take longer than conventional financing due to the involvement of multiple parties. During this phase, you should also begin assembling your documentation, including tax returns, financial statements, business plans, and any other materials required by the lender and CDC. Being proactive at this stage can significantly reduce delays later in the process.

After the purchase agreement is executed, the formal application process begins. This is where you submit a complete loan package to both the lender and the CDC. The lender typically takes the lead on underwriting, analyzing your creditworthiness, cash flow, and overall risk profile. The CDC focuses on the SBA portion of the loan, ensuring that your project meets all program requirements and aligns with economic development goals. While this may seem like a dual process, it is actually a coordinated effort, with both parties working together to move your loan toward approval.

Underwriting is one of the most critical phases of the SBA 504 loan process. During this stage, the lender conducts a detailed analysis of your financials, including income statements, balance sheets, and cash flow projections. They will calculate key metrics such as your debt service coverage ratio, liquidity, and leverage. They will also review your personal financial statement to assess your overall financial strength and ability to support the loan if needed. At the same time, the property itself is evaluated through an appraisal, environmental reports, and sometimes feasibility studies, depending on the nature of the project.

The appraisal is particularly important because it determines the value of the property and ensures that it supports the loan amount. If the appraisal comes in lower than expected, it can impact the loan structure and potentially require additional equity from the borrower. Environmental reports are also critical, especially for properties with potential contamination risks. These reports protect both the borrower and the lender by identifying any environmental issues that could affect the property's value or usability.

Once underwriting is complete, the loan moves to the approval stage. The lender issues a loan commitment outlining the terms and conditions of the bank portion of the financing. The CDC submits the project to the SBA for authorization of the debenture. This step involves a thorough review to ensure that all program requirements are met. Once approved, you receive a formal commitment that allows you to move forward with confidence.

The closing process for an SBA 504 loan occurs in two phases, which is another unique aspect of this program. The first phase is the closing of the bank loan, which provides the initial funding needed to acquire the property. The second phase is the funding of the CDC debenture, which typically occurs several weeks after the initial closing. During this interim period, the bank may provide bridge financing to cover the CDC portion until the debenture is funded. Understanding this two-step process is essential for managing expectations and ensuring that you have the necessary liquidity during the transition.

During closing, you will finalize all legal documents, including loan agreements, promissory notes, and security instruments. You will also fund your equity injection and cover closing costs, which may include appraisal fees, legal fees, and CDC fees. Once everything is signed and funded, ownership of the property is transferred, and your SBA 504 loan is officially in place.

One of the most important aspects of the SBA 504 loan process is communication and coordination. Because multiple parties are involved, including the borrower, lender, CDC, SBA, and various third-party providers, delays can occur if communication breaks down. Staying organized, responding promptly to requests, and working with experienced professionals can significantly improve your experience and reduce the likelihood of delays.

Another key factor in successfully navigating the SBA 504 loan process is preparation. The more organized and complete your documentation is, the smoother the process will be. This includes having up-to-date financial statements, clear explanations for any anomalies, and a well-thought-out business plan that demonstrates your ability to succeed. Preparation not only speeds up the process but also strengthens your position as a borrower.

As you move through the SBA 504 loan process, it is important to maintain a long-term perspective. While the process may seem complex and time-consuming, it is designed to ensure that you are entering into a stable and sustainable financing arrangement. The effort you invest upfront pays dividends over the life of the loan, providing you with predictable payments, strong cash flow, and the ability to build equity in a valuable asset.

By mastering the SBA 504 loan process, you gain more than just access to financing—you gain the ability to execute deals with confidence and precision. This knowledge allows you to move quickly when opportunities arise, avoid common pitfalls, and position yourself as a sophisticated borrower in the commercial real estate market. In the next chapters, you will build on this foundation by exploring advanced structuring techniques and strategies that will take your SBA 504 expertise to an even higher level.

Real-Life Math Example: Timeline, Costs, and Financial Impact of the SBA 504 Loan Process

To truly understand how the SBA 504 loan process works in real life, let's walk through a detailed example involving a borrower named Angela, who is purchasing a commercial office building for her expanding consulting firm. The purchase price of the property is $2,500,000, and Angela plans to occupy 65 percent of the building while leasing out the remaining space.

The process begins with prequalification, where Angela's financials are reviewed. Her business generates $400,000 in annual net operating income, and her personal credit score is strong. Based on this information, she receives a preliminary indication that she qualifies for an SBA 504 loan. This allows her to confidently move forward with submitting an offer on the property.

Angela negotiates a purchase agreement with a 90-day closing timeline, which provides sufficient time for the SBA loan process. She then submits her formal application, including tax returns, financial statements, and a business plan. The lender begins underwriting, while the CDC prepares the SBA portion of the loan.

The loan structure is as follows: the bank provides 50 percent of the purchase price, or $1,250,000, at an interest rate of 6.75 percent. The CDC provides 40 percent, or $1,000,000, at a fixed rate of 5.75 percent. Angela contributes 10 percent, or $250,000, as her equity injection.

During underwriting, an appraisal is conducted, confirming the property value at $2,500,000. Environmental reports show no issues, and the loan moves to approval. The bank issues a commitment, and the SBA authorizes the CDC debenture.

Now let's examine the timeline and costs. The entire process takes approximately 75 days from application to closing. Angela incurs closing costs totaling $50,000, which includes appraisal fees, legal fees, CDC fees, and other associated costs.

While this may seem significant, it is relatively small compared to the long-term benefits of the loan.

At closing, Angela funds her $250,000 down payment and covers the closing costs. The bank loan closes first, providing the funds needed to acquire the property. The CDC debenture is funded approximately 30 days later, at which point the bridge financing is replaced with the permanent SBA loan.

Now let's analyze the monthly payments. The bank loan of $1,250,000 results in a monthly payment of approximately $8,450. The CDC loan of $1,000,000 results in a monthly payment of approximately $6,100. The total monthly debt service is $14,550.

Angela leases out 35 percent of the building for $6,000 per month, or $72,000 annually. This reduces her effective monthly cost to $8,550. Previously, she was paying $12,000 per month in rent, meaning she saves $3,450 per month while also building equity in the property.

Over a 10-year period, the financial impact becomes even more compelling. Assuming a 3 percent annual appreciation rate, the property value increases to approximately $3,360,000. At the same time, Angela's loan balance decreases significantly, resulting in substantial equity. This equity can be leveraged for future investments, allowing her to scale her business and real estate portfolio.

This example illustrates how the SBA 504 loan process, while detailed, leads to powerful financial outcomes. By understanding the timeline, costs, and structure, Angela is able to navigate the process efficiently, secure favorable financing, and position herself for long-term success. The key takeaway is that mastering the process is just as important as understanding the loan itself, as it enables you to execute deals with confidence and precision.

Chapter 4

Structuring the SBA 504 Loan for Maximum Leverage, Cash Flow, and Long-Term Wealth

Once you understand the SBA 504 loan structure, eligibility requirements, and process, the next step is learning how to strategically structure your deal to maximize leverage, improve cash flow, and accelerate long-term wealth creation. This is where sophisticated borrowers separate themselves from average borrowers. The SBA 504 loan is not just a financing tool—it is a strategic framework that, when used correctly, allows you to control high-value assets, minimize upfront capital, and create multiple layers of financial benefit over time. In this chapter, you will learn how to structure SBA 504 deals intentionally so that every decision you make contributes to your long-term financial goals.

The first and most important concept in structuring an SBA 504 loan is leverage. Leverage is the ability to control a large asset with a relatively small amount of your own capital. In a traditional commercial loan, you may be required to put down 20 to 30 percent, which significantly limits your ability to scale. With an SBA 504 loan, that requirement is often reduced to 10 percent, allowing you to acquire more property with less money. This means that instead of tying up your capital in a single deal, you can preserve liquidity and position yourself to pursue additional opportunities.

However, leverage must be used intelligently. While a lower down payment increases your return on investment, it also increases your debt obligations. This is why cash flow becomes the second critical component of deal structuring. A well-structured SBA 504 deal should not only allow you to acquire the property but also generate positive or at least manageable cash flow from day one. This requires careful analysis of your monthly debt service, operating expenses, and any potential income from the property.

One of the most effective ways to improve cash flow in an SBA 504 deal is by incorporating rental income. Even though the program requires owner-occupancy, it still allows you to lease out a portion of the property. By doing so, you can offset your debt payments and reduce your effective occupancy cost. This strategy is especially powerful when you acquire a property that is slightly larger than your current needs, allowing you to grow into the space over time while generating income in the meantime. Another key element of structuring is selecting the right property. Not all properties are created equal, and the property you choose can significantly impact your financing, cash flow, and long-term appreciation. Ideally, you want a property that not only meets your operational needs but also has strong market demand, potential for appreciation, and the ability to generate additional income. This may include properties in growing areas, buildings with flexible layouts, or assets that can be improved to increase value.

The concept of total project cost is also critical in SBA 504 structuring. The loan is not limited to the purchase price of the property—it can also include renovation costs, construction expenses, equipment purchases, and certain soft costs. By including these elements in your project, you can finance a more comprehensive solution without having to come out of pocket for additional expenses. This allows you to acquire and improve a property in a single transaction, increasing its value and functionality from the start.

Timing is another strategic factor that can influence the success of your SBA 504 deal. Interest rates, market conditions, and economic trends all play a role in determining the optimal time to acquire property. While it is impossible to predict the market perfectly, understanding these factors allows you to make more informed decisions. For example, locking in a long-term fixed rate during a favorable rate environment can provide significant financial benefits over the life of the loan. In addition to timing, you must also consider your long-term exit strategy. While the SBA 504 loan is designed for long-term ownership, it is important to think about how the property fits into your overall financial plan. This may include holding the property for cash flow, refinancing in the future, or eventually selling the asset at a profit. By considering your exit strategy upfront, you can structure your deal in a way that maximizes flexibility and aligns with your goals.

Another advanced structuring strategy involves layering your financing with additional capital sources. While the SBA 504 loan covers a significant portion of the project cost, you may also have access to other forms of capital, such as business lines of credit, investor partnerships, or retained earnings. By strategically combining these resources, you can reduce your out-of-pocket investment, fund additional improvements, or accelerate your growth.

Risk management is also a crucial component of deal structuring. Every investment carries some level of risk, and it is your responsibility to identify and mitigate those risks as much as possible. This includes conducting thorough due diligence on the property, analyzing market conditions, and ensuring that your business has the capacity to support the loan. It also means building in a margin of safety in your financial projections, so you are prepared for unexpected changes in revenue or expenses. One often overlooked aspect of structuring is the psychological advantage of ownership. When you own your property, you are no longer subject to the uncertainties of leasing, such as rent increases or lease renewals. This stability allows you to focus on growing your business and executing your strategy without external disruptions. It also provides a sense of control and confidence that can have a significant impact on your decision-making and overall performance.

As you begin to structure SBA 504 deals, you will start to see patterns and opportunities that others may miss. You will learn how to identify properties that offer both operational and financial benefits, how to structure financing to maximize efficiency, and how to position yourself for long-term success. This level of expertise does not come from simply understanding the program—it comes from applying it strategically and consistently.

Ultimately, structuring an SBA 504 loan is about aligning your financing with your vision. It is about using the tools available to you to create opportunities, build wealth, and achieve your goals. By mastering the concepts in this chapter, you will be able to approach each deal with clarity, confidence, and a strategic mindset that sets you apart from the competition.

Real-Life Math Example: Structuring an SBA 504 Deal for Maximum Leverage and Cash Flow

Let's walk through a detailed real-life example to see how strategic structuring can dramatically impact the outcome of an SBA 504 deal. In this scenario, we will follow a borrower named Kevin, who owns a growing distribution company and is looking to purchase a commercial property to support his expansion.

Kevin identifies a property priced at $4,000,000. The building includes warehouse space, office areas, and additional units that can be leased to other businesses. Instead of pursuing a traditional loan requiring a 25 percent down payment of $1,000,000, Kevin uses an SBA 504 loan to reduce his upfront investment.

The loan is structured as follows: the bank provides 50 percent, or $2,000,000, at an interest rate of 6.75 percent. The CDC provides 40 percent, or $1,600,000, at a fixed rate of 5.75 percent. Kevin contributes 10 percent, or $400,000, as his down payment. Immediately, Kevin saves $600,000 compared to a traditional loan, which he can use for business growth and reserves.

Now let's analyze the monthly payments. The bank loan results in a monthly payment of approximately $13,500. The CDC loan results in a monthly payment of approximately $9,750. The total monthly debt service is $23,250.

Kevin plans to occupy 60 percent of the building and lease out the remaining 40 percent. He secures tenants who pay a combined total of $12,000 per month in rent. This rental income reduces his effective monthly cost to $11,250.

Before purchasing the property, Kevin was leasing space for $18,000 per month. By acquiring the property, he reduces his monthly occupancy cost by $6,750 while also building equity. Over the course of a year, this results in savings of $81,000, which can be reinvested into his business.

Now let's examine the long-term impact. Assuming the property appreciates at 3 percent annually, its value increases to approximately $5,372,000 after 10 years. At the same time, Kevin's loan balance decreases due to principal payments. If his total loan balance drops to around $3,000,000 after 10 years, he would have over $2,300,000 in equity.

In addition to appreciation and loan amortization, Kevin also benefits from rental income. Over 10 years, the $12,000 monthly rent generates $1,440,000 in total income. Even after accounting for expenses, this represents a significant financial advantage that further enhances his return on investment. Finally, let's calculate Kevin's return on his initial investment.

He invested $400,000 as a down payment. After 10 years, he has over $2,300,000 in equity, plus the financial benefits of reduced occupancy costs and rental income. This represents a return that far exceeds what he could have achieved with a traditional loan or by continuing to lease.

This example demonstrates how strategic structuring of an SBA 504 loan can transform a deal. By leveraging the program's advantages, Kevin is able to reduce his upfront investment, improve his cash flow, generate additional income, and build substantial long-term wealth. The key is to approach each deal with a strategic mindset, using the SBA 504 structure not just as a financing tool, but as a foundation for growth and success.

Chapter 5

Cash Flow Optimization, Expense Control, and Profit Maximization with SBA 504 Mortgage Loans

Once you have successfully structured and closed an SBA 504 loan, the real opportunity begins. Ownership alone does not create wealth—cash flow, expense management, and long-term financial discipline do. This chapter focuses on how to optimize the financial performance of your SBA 504-financed property so that it not only supports your business operations but also becomes a powerful income-producing asset. The goal is to move beyond simply owning real estate and into actively managing it as a profit center that contributes to your overall financial growth.

Cash flow is the lifeblood of any successful real estate investment, and with an SBA 504 loan, it is especially important because you are typically operating a business within the property while also managing debt obligations. The key is to ensure that your property either reduces your current expenses or generates additional income—or ideally, both. This begins with a clear understanding of your total monthly cost, which includes your mortgage payments, property taxes, insurance, maintenance, and any operational expenses associated with the property.

One of the most effective ways to optimize cash flow is by comparing your ownership costs to your previous leasing costs. Many business owners enter SBA 504 deals because they are tired of rising rents and lack of control. By transitioning from leasing to owning, you often stabilize or even reduce your monthly occupancy cost. However, the real advantage comes when you structure your property in a way that generates additional income, such as leasing unused space to other tenants. This creates a dual benefit: you reduce your own cost while creating a new revenue stream.

Expense control is equally important in maximizing profitability. Unlike leasing, where many costs are bundled into a single rent payment, ownership requires you to actively manage multiple expense categories. This includes property taxes, insurance premiums, maintenance, utilities, and repairs. By carefully monitoring and controlling these expenses, you can significantly improve your net cash flow. This may involve negotiating service contracts, implementing energy-efficient upgrades, or proactively maintaining the property to avoid costly repairs. Another key strategy for optimizing cash flow is increasing the efficiency of your space. Many properties have underutilized areas that can be repurposed or leased to generate additional income. For example, unused office space can be converted into rentable units, storage areas can be leased to third parties, or shared spaces can be monetized through flexible leasing arrangements. The goal is to ensure that every square foot of your property is either contributing to your business operations or generating income.

As you manage your property over time, you will also have opportunities to increase revenue through rent adjustments. If you have tenants in your building, periodic rent increases aligned with market conditions can significantly enhance your cash flow. Even small increases, when applied consistently over time, can have a substantial impact on your overall profitability. This is particularly powerful when combined with a fixed-rate SBA 504 loan, as your debt service remains stable while your income increases.

Another important aspect of profit maximization is understanding the tax benefits associated with owning commercial real estate. While this book does not provide tax advice, it is important to recognize that ownership often comes with advantages such as depreciation, interest deductions, and expense write-offs. These benefits can reduce your taxable income and improve your overall financial position. Working with a knowledgeable accountant or tax advisor can help you fully leverage these opportunities. Long-term planning is also critical when optimizing cash flow. The SBA 504 loan is designed for long-term ownership, which means you should be thinking several years ahead. This includes planning for future maintenance, potential expansions, and changes in your business operations. By anticipating these factors, you can make proactive decisions that protect your cash flow and ensure the sustainability of your investment.

One of the most powerful aspects of SBA 504 financing is the ability to create predictable financial outcomes. Because a significant portion of your loan is fixed-rate, your monthly payments remain stable over time. This allows you to plan with confidence and focus on increasing your income rather than worrying about rising costs. As inflation increases and market rents rise, your fixed payment becomes increasingly advantageous, effectively improving your cash flow year after year.

Another advanced strategy for maximizing profitability is reinvesting your savings. If your SBA 504 loan reduces your monthly occupancy cost compared to leasing, the difference can be reinvested into your business or additional investments. This could include hiring new employees, expanding your operations, or acquiring additional properties. By reinvesting strategically, you can accelerate your growth and multiply the benefits of your initial investment. Risk management also plays a role in maintaining strong cash flow. Unexpected expenses, vacancies, or economic changes can impact your financial performance. Building a reserve fund and maintaining conservative financial projections can help you navigate these challenges without disrupting your operations. The goal is to create a financial cushion that allows you to absorb short-term fluctuations while maintaining long-term stability.

Over time, as your loan balance decreases and your property value increases, your equity grows. This equity can be leveraged to access additional capital through refinancing or other financing strategies. This creates a cycle of growth, where one successful investment leads to another. By managing your cash flow effectively, you position yourself to take advantage of these opportunities and continue building wealth.

Ultimately, cash flow optimization is about taking control of your financial future. It is about turning your property into a strategic asset that supports your business, generates income, and creates long-term value. By applying the principles in this chapter, you will be able to maximize the benefits of your SBA 504 loan and transform your property into a powerful engine for growth and profitability.

Real-Life Math Example: Optimizing Cash Flow and Maximizing Profit with an SBA 504 Property

Let's walk through a detailed real-life example to illustrate how cash flow optimization and expense control can dramatically impact the profitability of an SBA 504-financed property. In this scenario, we will follow a borrower named Lisa, who owns a medical practice and is purchasing a commercial building to house her operations.

Lisa identifies a property priced at $3,500,000. Using an SBA 504 loan, the financing is structured with a 10 percent down payment of $350,000, a bank loan of $1,750,000 at 6.75 percent, and a CDC loan of $1,400,000 at 5.75 percent. Her total monthly debt service is approximately $20,350.

Before purchasing the property, Lisa was leasing space for $22,000 per month. At first glance, her new mortgage payment appears slightly lower, saving her $1,650 per month. However, the real opportunity lies in how she structures and manages the property after acquisition.

Lisa occupies 55 percent of the building for her medical practice and leases out the remaining 45 percent to complementary healthcare providers. She generates $14,000 per month in rental income, or $168,000 annually. This rental income reduces her effective monthly cost from $20,350 to just $6,350.

Now let's factor in operating expenses. Lisa spends approximately $4,000 per month on property taxes, insurance, maintenance, and utilities. This brings her total effective monthly cost to $10,350. Compared to her previous lease of $22,000, she is now saving $11,650 per month.

Over the course of a year, these savings add up to $139,800. Lisa decides to reinvest this money into her business, hiring additional staff and expanding her services. This leads to increased revenue, further strengthening her financial position.

Next, let's examine the long-term impact. Assuming the property appreciates at 3 percent annually, its value increases to approximately $4,703,000 after 10 years. During the same period, Lisa's loan balance decreases significantly due to principal payments. If her remaining loan balance is approximately $2,600,000 after 10 years, she would have over $2,100,000 in equity.

In addition to equity growth, Lisa benefits from consistent rental income. Over 10 years, the $14,000 monthly rent generates $1,680,000 in total income. Even after accounting for expenses and potential vacancies, this represents a substantial financial advantage.

Now let's calculate Lisa's return on investment. She initially invested $350,000 as a down payment. After 10 years, she has over $2,100,000 in equity, plus significant savings from reduced occupancy costs and rental income. This represents a return that far exceeds traditional investment options.

This example demonstrates how powerful cash flow optimization can be when combined with an SBA 504 loan. By strategically managing her property, controlling expenses, and maximizing income, Lisa transforms her real estate purchase into a highly profitable investment. The key is not just acquiring the property, but actively managing it in a way that enhances its financial performance over time.

Chapter 6

Long-Term Wealth Building, Equity Growth, and Exit Strategies with SBA 504 Mortgage Loans

When most borrowers first approach an SBA 504 loan, their primary focus is on acquisition—getting approved, securing the property, and stabilizing their business operations. However, the true power of the SBA 504 loan is not realized at closing, but over time. This chapter is dedicated to helping you understand how to transform your SBA 504-financed property into a long-term wealth-building asset by leveraging equity growth, strategic planning, and well-timed exit strategies.

The concept of long-term wealth in commercial real estate is built on three foundational pillars: loan amortization, property appreciation, and income generation. When these three elements work together, they create a compounding effect that can dramatically increase your net worth over time. The SBA 504 loan is uniquely positioned to support this process because it combines long-term fixed-rate financing with relatively low upfront capital requirements, allowing you to hold assets longer and benefit from these compounding forces. Loan amortization is one of the most powerful yet often overlooked components of wealth building. Every time you make a mortgage payment, a portion of that payment goes toward reducing your principal balance. Over time, this gradual reduction in debt increases your equity in the property. Unlike rent payments, which provide no long-term benefit, mortgage payments effectively convert your monthly expenses into ownership. With an SBA 504 loan, the long-term amortization schedule ensures that you are steadily building equity over a 20 to 25-year period.

Property appreciation is the second pillar of wealth creation. While real estate markets can fluctuate in the short term, commercial properties in strong locations tend to increase in value over time. Even modest annual appreciation can result in significant gains when applied over a long holding period. When combined with loan amortization, appreciation accelerates your equity growth, creating opportunities for refinancing, expansion, or eventual sale at a profit.

The third pillar, income generation, comes from both your business operations and any rental income associated with the property. If you are leasing out a portion of your building, that income not only offsets your expenses but also contributes to your overall return on investment. Over time, as rents increase and your loan payments remain fixed, your net income improves, further enhancing the financial performance of your investment. One of the most important concepts to understand in long-term wealth building is leverage. Because the SBA 504 loan allows you to acquire property with as little as 10 percent down, you are controlling a large asset with a relatively small amount of your own capital. This magnifies the impact of appreciation and income growth. For example, a 3 percent increase in property value may seem modest, but when applied to a multi-million-dollar asset, it can result in substantial gains relative to your initial investment.

As your equity grows, you gain access to new opportunities through refinancing or additional financing strategies. While SBA 504 loans are designed for long-term stability, there may come a time when refinancing becomes advantageous. This could be due to changes in interest rates, improvements in your financial position, or the desire to access equity for new investments. By refinancing strategically, you can unlock the value of your property without selling it, allowing you to continue benefiting from ownership while accessing additional capital.

Another key component of long-term strategy is portfolio expansion. Once you successfully complete one SBA 504 deal, you can use the knowledge, experience, and financial gains from that deal to pursue additional opportunities. This creates a cycle of growth, where each property contributes to your ability to acquire the next. Over time, this can lead to a diversified portfolio of commercial assets, each generating income and building equity.

Exit strategies are an essential part of this long-term planning. While the SBA 504 loan encourages long-term ownership, it is important to consider how and when you may eventually exit the investment. This could involve selling the property, refinancing and holding it for passive income, or transitioning it to another use. The key is to align your exit strategy with your financial goals and market conditions.

Selling the property can be a powerful way to realize the gains you have built over time. If your property has appreciated significantly and your loan balance has decreased, you may be able to sell at a substantial profit. This profit can then be reinvested into larger or more profitable opportunities, allowing you to scale your investments and accelerate your wealth-building journey.

Alternatively, you may choose to hold the property long-term and focus on cash flow. As your loan is paid down and eventually paid off, your monthly expenses decrease while your income continues. This creates a steady stream of passive income that can support your lifestyle, fund new investments, or provide financial security. Another advanced strategy involves repositioning the property to increase its value. This could include renovations, rebranding, or changing the tenant mix to attract higher-paying tenants. By increasing the property's income potential, you can significantly enhance its market value, creating additional equity and improving your overall return.

Risk management remains important throughout this process. Market conditions, economic changes, and business performance can all impact your investment. By maintaining a conservative approach, building reserves, and staying informed about market trends, you can navigate these challenges and protect your long-term gains.

The psychological aspect of long-term ownership should not be overlooked. As your equity grows and your financial position strengthens, you gain confidence and control over your future. This allows you to make strategic decisions without being constrained by short-term pressures. It also positions you to take advantage of opportunities that others may not be able to pursue.

Ultimately, the SBA 504 loan is not just a financing tool—it is a foundation for building lasting wealth. By understanding how to leverage equity growth, manage your property effectively, and plan your exit strategies, you can transform a single investment into a powerful financial engine that supports your goals for years to come.

Real-Life Math Example: Long-Term Equity Growth and Exit Strategy with an SBA 504 Property

Let's walk through a detailed real-life example to illustrate how long-term wealth is built using an SBA 504 loan. In this scenario, we will follow a borrower named Robert, who owns a construction company and purchases a commercial property for $5,000,000.

Robert uses an SBA 504 loan with a 10 percent down payment of $500,000. The bank provides $2,500,000 at 6.75 percent, and the CDC provides $2,000,000 at 5.75 percent. His total monthly debt service is approximately $29,000.

Robert occupies 60 percent of the property and leases out the remaining 40 percent, generating $18,000 per month in rental income. This reduces his effective monthly cost to $11,000. Previously, he was paying $20,000 per month in rent, so he immediately improves his cash flow by $9,000 per month.

Now let's examine the long-term impact over a 10-year period. Assuming the property appreciates at 3 percent annually, its value increases to approximately $6,720,000. During the same period, Robert's loan balance decreases significantly due to amortization. If his remaining loan balance is approximately $3,800,000 after 10 years, he has built $2,920,000 in equity.

In addition to equity growth, Robert generates rental income of $18,000 per month, or $216,000 per year. Over 10 years, this totals $2,160,000 in rental income. Even after accounting for expenses, this represents a substantial financial benefit.

Now let's consider an exit strategy. If Robert decides to sell the property after 10 years for $6,720,000, he would pay off his remaining loan balance of $3,800,000, leaving him with approximately $2,920,000 before transaction costs. Compared to his initial investment of $500,000, this represents a gain of over $2,400,000.

Alternatively, Robert could choose to refinance the property instead of selling. If he refinances based on the new value, he may be able to access a portion of his equity while continuing to own the property. This allows him to reinvest in new opportunities without giving up the income and appreciation potential of the original asset.

Finally, if Robert holds the property long-term and eventually pays off the loan, his monthly income increases dramatically. With no mortgage payments, the $18,000 monthly rental income becomes largely profit, creating a strong passive income stream.

This example demonstrates how the SBA 504 loan can be used not just to acquire property, but to build long-term wealth through equity growth, income generation, and strategic decision-making. By thinking beyond the initial purchase and focusing on the long-term potential, you can create a financial future that is both stable and scalable.

Chapter 7

Avoiding Costly Mistakes, Managing Risk, and Protecting Your SBA 504 Investment

As powerful as the SBA 504 loan is, it is not immune to risk. In fact, many borrowers who fail with commercial real estate do not fail because the program is flawed—they fail because of poor decisions, lack of preparation, or mismanagement after closing. This chapter is designed to help you identify, avoid, and mitigate the most common and costly mistakes associated with SBA 504 loans, while also building a risk management strategy that protects your investment and positions you for long-term success.

One of the most common mistakes borrowers make is overestimating their financial capacity. It is easy to become excited about acquiring a large commercial property, especially when the SBA 504 loan allows for a low down payment. However, just because you can qualify for a certain loan amount does not mean you should take on that level of debt. The key is to ensure that your business can comfortably support the loan under both normal and stressed conditions. This means analyzing not only your current cash flow, but also potential scenarios such as reduced revenue, increased expenses, or temporary vacancies.

Another major mistake is underestimating operating expenses. Many first-time property owners focus heavily on the mortgage payment but overlook the full cost of ownership. Property taxes, insurance, maintenance, repairs, utilities, and unexpected capital expenditures can add up quickly. If these costs are not properly accounted for, they can erode your cash flow and create financial strain. A disciplined approach to budgeting, along with conservative estimates, is essential for maintaining stability.

Poor property selection is another critical risk factor. Not all properties are good investments, even if they qualify for SBA 504 financing. A property in a declining area, with limited demand, or with structural issues can become a liability rather than an asset. It is essential to conduct thorough due diligence, including market analysis, property inspections, and evaluation of future growth potential. The goal is to select a property that not only meets your current needs but also has long-term value and flexibility.

Another common pitfall is failing to plan for vacancies. Even if you intend to occupy the majority of the property, any leased space carries the risk of tenant turnover. If a tenant leaves and the space remains vacant for an extended period, your rental income decreases while your expenses remain the same. This can significantly impact your cash flow. Building a reserve fund and maintaining conservative projections can help you navigate these periods without financial stress.

Interest rate risk is often less of a concern with SBA 504 loans due to the fixed-rate CDC portion, but it is still important to understand the overall structure. The bank portion of the loan may have different terms, including potential rate adjustments or refinancing requirements. Understanding these details and planning accordingly ensures that you are not caught off guard in the future.

Another mistake borrowers make is failing to maintain proper financial documentation and organization. Lenders, CDCs, and even future buyers or refinancing partners will require clear and accurate records of your financial performance. Keeping detailed records of income, expenses, leases, and maintenance not only helps you manage your property effectively but also strengthens your position for future opportunities.

Overleveraging is another risk that must be managed carefully. While the SBA 504 loan allows for high leverage, taking on too much debt can limit your flexibility and increase your exposure to financial stress. It is important to strike a balance between maximizing leverage and maintaining a comfortable financial cushion. This includes having sufficient reserves, manageable debt service, and a clear plan for handling unexpected challenges.

One often overlooked risk is the operational risk associated with your business. Because SBA 504 loans require owner-occupancy, your business performance is directly tied to your ability to maintain the property. If your business experiences a downturn, it can impact your ability to meet your loan obligations. This makes it essential to maintain a strong and diversified business model, as well as contingency plans for different scenarios.

Another important consideration is compliance with SBA requirements. The SBA 504 program has specific rules regarding occupancy, use of funds, and ongoing operations. Failing to comply with these requirements can lead to complications, including potential penalties or issues with your loan. Staying informed and working with experienced professionals can help ensure that you remain in compliance throughout the life of the loan.

Insurance and risk mitigation strategies are also critical components of protecting your investment. This includes not only property insurance but also liability coverage and business interruption insurance. These policies provide a safety net in the event of unexpected events such as natural disasters, accidents, or operational disruptions. While insurance represents an additional cost, it is a necessary investment in protecting your long-term financial stability.

Another advanced risk management strategy involves stress testing your investment. This means analyzing how your deal performs under different scenarios, such as a 20 percent drop in revenue, a period of vacancy, or an increase in expenses. By understanding these potential outcomes, you can identify weaknesses in your deal and make adjustments before they become real problems.

As you gain experience with SBA 504 loans, you will begin to develop a more refined approach to risk management. You will learn how to identify red flags, structure deals more conservatively, and make decisions that prioritize long-term stability over short-term gains. This mindset is essential for building a sustainable real estate portfolio and avoiding the mistakes that derail many investors.

Ultimately, avoiding costly mistakes and managing risk is about discipline, preparation, and awareness. It is about understanding that every decision you make has consequences and that success in commercial real estate requires both strategic thinking and careful execution. By applying the principles in this chapter, you can protect your investment, minimize your risks, and position yourself for long-term success with SBA 504 financing.

Real-Life Math Example: Stress Testing and Risk Management in an SBA 504 Investment

To fully understand how risk management works in practice, let's walk through a detailed example involving a borrower named Daniel, who owns a service-based business and purchases a commercial property for $3,800,000 using an SBA 504 loan.

Daniel's loan is structured with a 10 percent down payment of $380,000, a bank loan of $1,900,000 at 6.75 percent, and a CDC loan of $1,520,000 at 5.75 percent. His total monthly debt service is approximately $22,000. Daniel occupies 60 percent of the property and leases out the remaining 40 percent, generating $10,000 per month in rental income.

At baseline, Daniel's effective monthly cost is $12,000 after accounting for rental income. His business generates sufficient cash flow to comfortably cover this amount, and the deal appears strong. However, to properly manage risk, Daniel conducts a stress test to evaluate different scenarios. First, Daniel considers a vacancy scenario where his tenants leave and he temporarily loses the $10,000 monthly rental income. In this case, his monthly cost increases to the full $22,000. If his business can still cover this amount, the deal remains stable. If not, he must rely on reserves or make adjustments to his operations.

Next, Daniel evaluates a revenue decline scenario where his business income decreases by 25 percent. If his original monthly net income was $30,000, a 25 percent decline reduces it to $22,500. With a full debt service of $22,000, his margin becomes extremely tight. This highlights the importance of maintaining reserves and avoiding overleveraging.

Daniel also analyzes an expense increase scenario. If property taxes, insurance, and maintenance increase by $3,000 per month, his effective cost rises accordingly. Combined with other stress factors, this could significantly impact his cash flow.

To prepare for these risks, Daniel sets aside a reserve fund of $150,000. This provides him with approximately seven months of full debt service coverage, giving him time to stabilize the property or adjust his business operations if needed.

Now let's examine the long-term impact under normal

conditions. Assuming the property appreciates at 3 percent annually, its value increases to approximately $5,104,000 after 10 years. During the same period, Daniel's loan balance decreases, resulting in significant equity growth.

However, the key takeaway from this example is not just the potential for profit, but the importance of preparation. By stress testing his deal and building reserves, Daniel is able to protect himself against potential risks and ensure the long-term success of his investment.

This example demonstrates that successful SBA 504 investing is not just about maximizing returns—it is about managing risk and maintaining stability. By understanding the numbers, planning for different scenarios, and making disciplined decisions, you can protect your investment and build a strong foundation for long-term wealth.

Chapter 8

Using SBA 504 Loans for Construction, Renovation, and Expansion Projects

One of the most powerful and often underutilized aspects of the SBA 504 loan program is its ability to finance not only the acquisition of commercial real estate, but also the construction, renovation, and expansion of business properties. While many borrowers initially think of SBA 504 loans strictly in terms of purchasing existing buildings, the program is equally effective—if not more powerful—when used to build or improve properties that are specifically tailored to a business's long-term needs. This chapter will guide you through how to strategically use SBA 504 financing for construction and expansion projects, allowing you to create custom-built assets that maximize operational efficiency and long-term value.

Construction projects present a unique opportunity because they allow you to design a property from the ground up. Instead of adapting your business to fit an existing building, you can create a space that is optimized for your operations, workflow, and future growth. This level of customization can lead to increased productivity, improved customer experience, and greater overall efficiency. However, construction projects also introduce additional complexity, including longer timelines, higher upfront costs, and increased risk. Understanding how to structure these projects within the SBA 504 framework is essential for success.

The SBA 504 loan can be used to finance ground-up construction, major renovations, or expansions of existing facilities. The total project cost can include land acquisition, construction costs, architectural and engineering fees, permits, and certain soft costs associated with the project. This comprehensive financing approach allows you to bundle all necessary expenses into a single loan structure, reducing the need for additional capital and simplifying the financing process.

One of the key differences between acquisition and construction projects is the timeline. While purchasing an existing property may take a few months, construction projects can take a year or more to complete. During this time, you may not be generating income from the property, which makes it essential to plan your cash flow carefully. Many lenders provide interest-only payments during the construction phase, which helps reduce the financial burden while the project is being completed. Once construction is finished, the loan transitions into permanent financing with full principal and interest payments. Another important consideration is contingency planning. Construction projects often encounter unexpected challenges, such as cost overruns, delays, or changes in scope. Including a contingency reserve in your project budget is critical for managing these uncertainties. This reserve typically ranges from 5 to 10 percent of the total project cost and provides a financial cushion that allows you to address issues without disrupting the project.

The SBA 504 structure for construction projects remains similar to that of acquisition deals, with a bank providing approximately 50 percent of the financing, the CDC providing up to 40 percent, and the borrower contributing the remaining portion. However, because construction projects carry higher risk, lenders may require additional documentation, stronger financials, or higher equity contributions in certain cases. This makes preparation and planning even more important.

Renovation projects offer another powerful opportunity to create value. By acquiring a property that may be outdated or underutilized and investing in improvements, you can significantly increase its functionality and market value. This may include upgrading systems, reconfiguring layouts, or enhancing the property's appearance to attract higher-quality tenants. The ability to finance these improvements through an SBA 504 loan allows you to execute your vision without depleting your working capital. Expansion projects are particularly relevant for growing businesses that have outgrown their current space. Instead of relocating to a new property, you may be able to expand your existing facility, adding square footage or improving infrastructure to support increased operations. This approach allows you to maintain continuity while scaling your business, reducing disruption and preserving your existing customer base.

Another key advantage of using SBA 504 loans for construction and expansion is the ability to lock in long-term financing from the outset. Unlike short-term construction loans that require refinancing upon completion, the SBA 504 program provides a clear path to permanent financing. This eliminates the uncertainty associated with future interest rates and refinancing conditions, allowing you to plan your finances with confidence.

Site selection is a critical component of any construction or expansion project. The location of your property can significantly impact its long-term success, influencing factors such as customer access, employee convenience, and property value. Conducting thorough market research and selecting a site with strong growth potential is essential for maximizing your return on investment.

Project management is another important factor in ensuring

the success of construction and renovation projects. This includes coordinating with contractors, managing timelines, and ensuring that the project stays within budget. Working with experienced professionals and maintaining clear communication throughout the process can help prevent delays and cost overruns.

As you complete your construction or renovation project, you transition into the operational phase, where the focus shifts to maximizing the value of your newly improved property. This includes optimizing your space, generating income from any leasable areas, and managing expenses effectively. The goal is to ensure that your investment delivers both operational benefits and financial returns.

Ultimately, using SBA 504 loans for construction, renovation, and expansion allows you to take control of your business environment and create assets that are tailored to your needs. By understanding the unique considerations associated with these projects and applying strategic planning, you can unlock opportunities that go beyond simple property acquisition and position yourself for long-term growth and success.

Real-Life Math Example: SBA 504 Construction Project with Expansion and Value Creation

Let's walk through a detailed real-life example to illustrate how an SBA 504 loan can be used to finance a construction and expansion project. In this scenario, we will follow a borrower named Sophia, who owns a rapidly growing fitness and wellness company.

Sophia currently leases multiple locations and wants to consolidate her operations into a single, custom-built facility. She identifies a piece of land for $800,000 and plans to construct a 20,000-square-foot building at a cost of $4,200,000. The total project cost, including soft costs and contingency reserves, is $5,200,000.

Using an SBA 504 loan, the financing is structured as follows: the bank provides 50 percent of the project cost, or $2,600,000, at an interest rate of 6.75 percent. The CDC provides 40 percent, or $2,080,000, at a fixed rate of 5.75 percent. Sophia contributes 10 percent, or $520,000, as her equity injection.

During the construction phase, Sophia makes interest-only payments on the bank portion of the loan, which amount to approximately $14,600 per month. This allows her to manage her cash flow while the facility is being built. Once construction is complete, the loan converts to full principal and interest payments, with a total monthly debt service of approximately $30,200.

Sophia plans to occupy 65 percent of the building and lease out the remaining 35 percent to complementary businesses such as physical therapists, nutritionists, and wellness providers. She generates $15,000 per month in rental income, which reduces her effective monthly cost to $15,200.

Before this project, Sophia was paying a combined total of $22,000 per month in rent across multiple locations. By consolidating into her own facility, she not only reduces her monthly cost by $6,800 but also gains operational efficiency and control.

Now let's examine the long-term impact. Assuming the property appreciates at 3 percent annually, its value increases to approximately $6,990,000 after 10 years. During the same period, Sophia's loan balance decreases significantly, resulting in substantial equity.

In addition to appreciation, Sophia generates rental income of $15,000 per month, or $180,000 per year. Over 10 years, this totals $1,800,000 in income. Combined with her cost savings and increased business revenue from operating in a custom-built facility, the financial benefits are significant.

Finally, let's calculate Sophia's return on investment. She initially invested $520,000. After 10 years, she has built millions in equity, generated substantial rental income, and improved her business operations. This demonstrates how using an SBA 504 loan for construction and expansion can create both immediate and long-term financial advantages.

This example highlights the power of combining strategic planning with SBA 504 financing. By building a property tailored to her needs and leveraging the program's advantages, Sophia is able to transform her business and create a valuable long-term asset.

Chapter 9

SBA 504 Loan Terms, Interest Rates, Fees, and How to Compare Financing Options

To truly master SBA 504 mortgage loans, you must understand not just how they work structurally, but how the numbers behind them impact your long-term financial outcomes. Interest rates, fees, loan terms, and repayment structures all play a critical role in determining whether a deal is profitable, sustainable, and aligned with your goals. This chapter will break down each of these components in detail and show you how to compare SBA 504 loans with other financing options so you can consistently make the best decisions.

One of the defining characteristics of the SBA 504 loan is its dual-loan structure, which creates two different interest rate environments within the same deal. The bank portion, typically 50 percent of the project cost, may carry a fixed or variable interest rate depending on the lender and market conditions. The CDC portion, which typically covers up to 40 percent, is funded through a debenture and carries a long-term fixed interest rate, usually for 20 or 25 years. This combination creates a blended rate that is often more favorable than traditional commercial loans.

The CDC portion is particularly valuable because it provides stability. In a rising interest rate environment, having a significant portion of your loan locked in at a fixed rate protects you from future increases. This predictability allows you to plan your finances with confidence and ensures that your debt service remains manageable over time. For many borrowers, this is one of the most important advantages of the SBA 504 program.

The bank portion, on the other hand, introduces some variability. While many lenders offer fixed rates for a certain period, others may provide adjustable rates or shorter fixed terms with balloon payments. It is essential to fully understand the terms of the bank portion, including any potential rate adjustments, refinancing requirements, or prepayment penalties. These factors can significantly impact your long-term financial strategy.

Loan terms for SBA 504 financing are generally longer than those of traditional commercial loans. The CDC portion typically offers 20- or 25-year amortization, while the bank portion may range from 20 to 25 years as well. Longer amortization periods result in lower monthly payments, which improves cash flow and makes it easier to manage your finances. However, it is important to recognize that longer terms also mean more interest paid over time, which should be factored into your overall analysis.

Fees are another important component of SBA 504 loans. While the program offers many advantages, it also includes certain costs that must be considered. These may include CDC processing fees, SBA guaranty fees, legal fees, appraisal costs, and closing costs. Some of these fees can be financed into the loan, while others must be paid upfront. Understanding the full cost of the loan ensures that you are not surprised during the closing process and allows you to accurately evaluate the total investment.

Prepayment considerations are also critical. The CDC portion of the SBA 504 loan typically includes a declining prepayment penalty for the first 10 years. This penalty is designed to protect the investors who purchase the debentures and ensure stability in the program. While this may limit your ability to refinance or sell the property in the early years, it also reinforces the long-term nature of the loan. The bank portion may have its own prepayment terms, which vary by lender and should be carefully reviewed.

When comparing SBA 504 loans to other financing options, it is important to look beyond just the interest rate. While a traditional loan may offer a slightly lower rate in some cases, it often requires a higher down payment, shorter term, or variable rate structure. These factors can significantly impact your cash flow and long-term returns. The SBA 504 loan, with its lower equity requirement and fixed-rate component, often provides a more balanced and strategic financing solution.

For example, a traditional commercial loan may require a 25 percent down payment and offer a 10-year term with a balloon payment. While the initial rate may be competitive, the higher equity requirement limits your leverage, and the shorter term introduces refinancing risk. In contrast, the SBA 504 loan allows you to put down as little as 10 percent and provides long-term financing that reduces uncertainty and enhances stability.

Another important factor to consider is the effective cost of capital. This includes not only the interest rate and fees but also the opportunity cost of your down payment. By using an SBA 504 loan and preserving capital, you can invest that money elsewhere, potentially generating additional returns. This broader perspective allows you to evaluate financing options in a more strategic way.

Cash flow analysis is essential when comparing loans. A lower monthly payment can significantly improve your ability to manage expenses, reinvest in your business, and build reserves. Even if the total interest paid over time is higher, the improved cash flow can create opportunities that outweigh the additional cost. This is particularly important for growing businesses that need liquidity to expand.

Risk is another critical consideration. Loans with variable rates or short terms expose you to market fluctuations and refinancing uncertainty. The SBA 504 loan mitigates much of this risk through its fixed-rate component and long-term structure. This makes it an attractive option for borrowers who prioritize stability and predictability.

As you evaluate different financing options, it is important to align your decision with your long-term goals. If your objective is to minimize upfront costs, maximize leverage, and create stable cash flow, the SBA 504 loan is often the superior choice. If your strategy involves short-term ownership or rapid turnover, other financing options may be more appropriate. The key is to understand the trade-offs and make informed decisions.

Ultimately, mastering the terms, rates, and costs of SBA 504 loans allows you to approach each deal with clarity and confidence. It enables you to structure financing that supports your goals, avoid costly mistakes, and maximize your returns. By understanding how to compare options effectively, you position yourself as a strategic borrower who can consistently make smart financial decisions.

Real-Life Math Example: Comparing SBA 504 Loan vs Traditional Commercial Loan

To fully understand how SBA 504 loan terms and costs impact your financial outcome, let's walk through a detailed comparison between an SBA 504 loan and a traditional commercial loan. In this example, we will follow a borrower named Michael, who is purchasing a commercial property for $3,000,000.

First, let's look at the SBA 504 loan scenario. The financing is structured with a 10 percent down payment of $300,000. The bank provides $1,500,000 at 6.75 percent, and the CDC provides $1,200,000 at 5.75 percent. The total monthly debt service is approximately $17,400.

Now let's examine the traditional loan scenario. The lender requires a 25 percent down payment of $750,000 and provides a loan of $2,250,000 at 6.25 percent with a 20-year amortization and a 10-year balloon. The monthly payment is approximately $16,500.

At first glance, the traditional loan appears slightly more attractive due to the lower monthly payment and interest rate. However, the key difference lies in the equity requirement. Michael must invest an additional $450,000 upfront compared to the SBA 504 loan.

Now let's consider what Michael can do with that $450,000. If he invests it into his business or another opportunity that generates a 10 percent annual return, it would produce $45,000 per year. Over 10 years, this amounts to $450,000 in returns, effectively offsetting the higher monthly payment of the SBA 504 loan.

Next, let's analyze cash flow. Suppose Michael leases out a portion of the property and generates $8,000 per month in rental income. Under the SBA 504 scenario, his effective monthly cost is reduced to $9,400. Under the traditional loan, his effective cost is $8,500. The difference is relatively small, but the SBA 504 loan still provides the advantage of lower upfront capital.

Now let's examine long-term risk. The traditional loan includes a balloon payment after 10 years, which requires refinancing. If interest rates increase or market conditions change, Michael may face higher costs or difficulty refinancing. The SBA 504 loan, with its long-term fixed-rate component, eliminates this risk and provides greater stability.

Finally, let's consider equity growth. Assuming the property appreciates at 3 percent annually, it will be worth approximately $4,031,000 after 10 years. Under both scenarios, Michael builds equity through appreciation and loan amortization. However, because he invested less upfront in the SBA 504 loan, his return on investment is significantly higher.

This example demonstrates that while traditional loans may appear competitive on the surface, the SBA 504 loan often provides superior overall value when you consider leverage, opportunity cost, and long-term stability. By understanding how to analyze these factors, you can make informed decisions that align with your financial goals and maximize your returns.

Chapter 10

Advanced SBA 504 Deal Structuring and Building a Scalable Commercial Real Estate Strategy

By the time you reach this stage, you understand how SBA 504 loans work, how to qualify, how to structure deals, optimize cash flow, manage risk, and evaluate financing options. Now it is time to bring everything together into a higher-level strategy—one that allows you not just to complete a single successful transaction, but to build a scalable system for acquiring, managing, and growing a portfolio of commercial real estate assets using SBA 504 financing.

Advanced structuring begins with thinking beyond the individual deal and focusing on your long-term vision. Instead of asking, "Can I afford this property?" you begin asking, "How does this property fit into my 5-year and 10-year strategy?" This shift in thinking is what transforms borrowers into strategic investors. Every decision you make—from property selection to loan structure—should align with your broader goal of building wealth, increasing cash flow, and expanding your portfolio.

One of the most powerful strategies in SBA 504 financing is sequencing your deals. Because the program requires owner-occupancy, each property must be tied to an operating business. However, this does not limit your ability to scale—it simply requires strategic planning. As your business grows, you can acquire larger properties, move into new locations, or create separate operating entities that allow you to utilize SBA 504 financing multiple times. This approach enables you to build a portfolio over time while staying within program guidelines.

Another advanced strategy involves maximizing each property's potential before moving on to the next. This means fully optimizing cash flow, leasing unused space, improving operations, and increasing the value of the asset. By doing so, you strengthen your financial position and create a solid foundation for future acquisitions. Lenders and CDCs are more likely to support borrowers who demonstrate successful management of previous properties, making each completed deal a stepping stone to the next.

Entity structuring also plays a critical role in advanced SBA 504 strategies. Many experienced borrowers use separate legal entities for different properties and operations. This can provide liability protection, simplify accounting, and create flexibility for future transactions. For example, you may have one entity that operates your business and another that holds the real estate, with a lease agreement between them. This structure allows you to manage risk while maintaining control over both the business and the property.

Another key concept is capital recycling. As your properties appreciate and your loan balances decrease, you build equity that can be leveraged for new opportunities. While SBA 504 loans are not typically refinanced in the early years due to prepayment penalties, over time, you may be able to access this equity through other financing methods. This allows you to reinvest your gains and continue expanding your portfolio without relying solely on new capital.

Strategic partnerships can also accelerate your growth. By partnering with other business owners or investors, you can combine resources, share risk, and pursue larger opportunities. This may involve joint ventures, co-investment structures, or strategic alliances that allow you to scale more quickly than you could on your own. The key is to ensure that all parties are aligned in their goals and that the structure of the partnership supports long-term success.

Market selection is another critical factor in advanced deal structuring. Not all markets offer the same opportunities, and choosing the right location can significantly impact your results. This includes analyzing factors such as population growth, economic development, demand for commercial space, and local business trends. Investing in strong markets increases the likelihood of appreciation, stable occupancy, and long-term success.

Another advanced strategy is value-add investing. This involves acquiring properties that have untapped potential and implementing improvements that increase their value. This could include renovating outdated spaces, improving management, or repositioning the property to attract higher-quality tenants. By increasing the property's income and appeal, you can significantly enhance its value and create additional equity.

Timing your decisions is also important. This includes not only when you acquire a property, but also when you refinance, expand, or exit. Understanding market cycles and economic trends allows you to make more informed decisions and maximize your returns. While it is impossible to time the market perfectly, being aware of these factors can give you a strategic advantage.

Another key element of scaling your portfolio is building a strong team. This includes lenders, CDCs, real estate agents, attorneys, accountants, and property managers who understand your goals and can support your strategy. Having the right team in place allows you to move more efficiently, avoid mistakes, and take advantage of opportunities as they arise.

Technology and systems also play a role in advanced strategies. As your portfolio grows, managing multiple properties and transactions becomes more complex. Implementing systems for tracking finances, managing tenants, and monitoring performance can help you stay organized and make better decisions. This level of organization is essential for scaling successfully.

As you build your portfolio, it is important to maintain a disciplined approach. This means sticking to your criteria, avoiding overleveraging, and making decisions based on data rather than emotion. While opportunities may arise that seem attractive, not every deal is the right deal. Staying focused on your strategy ensures that you continue to move in the right direction.

Ultimately, advanced SBA 504 deal structuring is about creating a repeatable system for success. It is about using the program not just as a one-time solution, but as a long-term strategy for building wealth and achieving financial independence. By applying the principles in this chapter, you can move beyond individual transactions and begin building a scalable, sustainable commercial real estate portfolio.

Real-Life Math Example: Scaling an SBA 504 Portfolio Over 10 Years

Let's walk through a comprehensive example to illustrate how advanced structuring and strategic planning can be used to build a scalable portfolio using SBA 504 loans. In this scenario, we will follow a borrower named Anthony, who owns a growing service business and begins acquiring commercial properties over a 10-year period.

In year one, Anthony purchases his first property for $2,500,000 using an SBA 504 loan. He puts down 10 percent, or $250,000, while the bank and CDC finance the remaining $2,250,000. His monthly debt service is approximately $14,500, and he generates $5,000 per month in rental income, reducing his effective cost to $9,500.

Over the next three years, Anthony optimizes the property by increasing rental income to $7,000 per month and improving his business operations. The property appreciates at 3 percent annually, increasing its value to approximately $2,731,000. His loan balance decreases to around $2,100,000, giving him over $600,000 in equity.

In year four, Anthony uses his improved financial position to acquire a second property for $3,500,000. He invests $350,000 as a down payment and structures the deal similarly. This property generates $10,000 per month in rental income, further improving his overall cash flow.

By year seven, Anthony owns two properties with a combined value of approximately $6,800,000 and significant equity. His rental income has increased, and his business has grown, allowing him to pursue a third acquisition.

In year eight, he acquires a third property for $4,500,000 with a $450,000 down payment. This property generates $15,000 per month in rental income and further strengthens his portfolio.

By year ten, Anthony owns three properties with a combined value of approximately $11,000,000. His total equity across all properties exceeds $4,000,000, and his rental income generates over $30,000 per month.

Anthony's total initial investment across all three properties is $1,050,000. Over 10 years, he has built over $4,000,000 in equity and created a strong cash flow stream. This represents a significant return on investment and demonstrates the power of scaling with SBA 504 loans.

This example highlights how strategic planning, disciplined execution, and advanced structuring can transform a single SBA 504 loan into a scalable wealth-building system. By focusing on long-term growth and leveraging the program effectively, you can create a portfolio that generates income, builds equity, and provides financial independence.

Chapter 11

Building a Long-Term SBA 504 Acquisition Pipeline and Turning Deal Flow into Predictable Growth

At this stage, you are no longer thinking like a borrower completing a single transaction—you are thinking like an operator building a system. The difference between someone who completes one SBA 504 deal and someone who builds a multi-million-dollar portfolio is not just knowledge, but consistency. That consistency comes from creating a repeatable acquisition pipeline—a system that continuously generates opportunities, filters the best deals, and converts them into closed transactions. In this chapter, you will learn how to build that pipeline so that your growth becomes predictable rather than random.

The first principle of building a pipeline is understanding that deals do not appear—they are created. Most successful SBA 504 borrowers are not waiting for opportunities to come to them; they are actively generating them through relationships, marketing, and strategic positioning. This means you must become visible in your market as someone who buys, develops, or occupies commercial real estate. When brokers, business owners, and lenders know what you are looking for, they begin bringing opportunities to you.

One of the most powerful sources of deal flow is relationships with commercial real estate agents and brokers. These professionals are constantly exposed to properties that may not even be publicly listed. By building strong relationships with them and clearly communicating your criteria—such as property type, price range, occupancy needs, and location—you increase your chances of being presented with off-market or early-stage opportunities. The key is consistency. Regular communication keeps you top of mind.

Another important source of deals is direct outreach. Many property owners are open to selling but have not formally listed their properties. By reaching out directly—through mail campaigns, calls, or targeted marketing—you can uncover opportunities that others are not competing for. This approach requires effort and persistence, but it can lead to highly favorable deals because there is less competition.

Your existing network is also a valuable resource. Business owners, vendors, clients, and even competitors may know of properties or opportunities that align with your goals. By sharing your strategy and intentions with your network, you create additional channels for deal flow. Over time, this network effect can become a significant source of opportunities.

As your pipeline grows, the next step is filtering deals effectively. Not every opportunity is worth pursuing, and evaluating deals quickly and accurately is essential. This involves analyzing key metrics such as purchase price, projected cash flow, occupancy potential, and alignment with SBA 504 requirements. By developing clear criteria, you can quickly determine whether a deal is worth pursuing or should be passed on.

Speed is another critical factor in converting opportunities into closed deals. In competitive markets, the ability to move quickly can be the difference between securing a property and losing it to another buyer. This is where preparation becomes essential. Having your financial documents ready, maintaining strong relationships with lenders and CDCs, and understanding the SBA 504 process allows you to act decisively when the right opportunity arises.

Another important component of building a pipeline is tracking your opportunities. This can be done using simple tools such as spreadsheets or more advanced systems like CRM software. The goal is to monitor where each deal stands in the process, from initial contact to closing. This level of organization ensures that no opportunity is lost due to lack of follow-up or oversight. Consistency in your pipeline also requires a long-term mindset. Not every deal will close, and not every opportunity will work out. However, by maintaining a steady flow of potential deals, you increase your chances of consistently closing transactions. This approach reduces reliance on any single deal and creates a more stable and predictable growth pattern.

Marketing plays a significant role in building your pipeline. This includes positioning yourself as an expert in SBA 504 financing and commercial real estate. By creating content, sharing insights, and demonstrating your expertise, you attract opportunities and build credibility. This can be done through social media, websites, or direct communication with your network.

Another advanced strategy is targeting specific niches. Instead of looking at all types of properties, you may focus on a particular segment, such as medical offices, warehouses, or retail spaces. By specializing, you develop deeper knowledge and stronger relationships within that niche, which can lead to better opportunities and more efficient deal evaluation.

Timing also plays a role in pipeline development. Market conditions, interest rates, and economic trends can influence the availability and attractiveness of deals. By staying informed and adjusting your strategy accordingly, you can position yourself to take advantage of favorable conditions while avoiding unnecessary risks.

As your pipeline matures, you will begin to see patterns in your deals. You will identify which types of properties perform best, which markets offer the most opportunities, and which strategies yield the highest returns. This knowledge allows you to refine your approach and focus on the most effective methods.

Another key aspect of pipeline building is scalability. As your operations grow, you may need to delegate certain tasks, such as deal sourcing, analysis, or property management. Building a team or leveraging external resources allows you to handle a higher volume of opportunities without becoming overwhelmed.

The ultimate goal of building an SBA 504 acquisition pipeline is to create a system that produces consistent results. Instead of relying on luck or timing, you develop a structured approach that generates opportunities, filters them effectively, and converts them into successful deals. This transforms your real estate strategy from reactive to proactive.

By mastering this process, you position yourself for long-term growth and success. You move from completing individual transactions to building a sustainable business that continuously creates value. This is the foundation of a scalable commercial real estate strategy and the key to achieving financial independence through SBA 504 financing.

Real-Life Math Example: Building a Deal Pipeline and Converting Opportunities into Portfolio Growth

Let's walk through a detailed example to illustrate how building a consistent pipeline can lead to predictable growth using SBA 504 loans. In this scenario, we will follow a borrower named Carlos, who owns a service business and wants to acquire commercial properties over a 5-year period.

Carlos begins by setting a goal of acquiring one property per year. He builds relationships with three commercial brokers, launches a small direct mail campaign targeting property owners, and actively networks within his local business community. Over the course of a year, Carlos identifies 20 potential deals.

Out of these 20 deals, Carlos determines that 10 meet his basic criteria. He performs deeper analysis on these 10 deals and submits offers on 5 of them. Ultimately, he successfully closes on 1 property, which aligns with his goal.

The first property is purchased for $2,000,000 using an SBA 504 loan with a 10 percent down payment of $200,000. The property generates $4,000 per month in rental income, reducing his effective monthly cost and improving his cash flow.

In year two, Carlos repeats the process. His increased experience and credibility lead to 30 potential deals, 15 qualified opportunities, 7 offers, and 2 closed transactions. He acquires two additional properties for $2,500,000 and $3,000,000, investing a total of $550,000 in down payments.

By year three, Carlos has refined his pipeline and increased his efficiency. He reviews 40 deals, qualifies 20, submits 10 offers, and closes 2 more properties. His portfolio now includes five properties with a combined value of approximately $12,500,000.

Let's analyze the financial impact. Carlos's total investment over three years is approximately $1,300,000. His properties generate a combined rental income of $20,000 per month, or $240,000 per year. This income significantly offsets his debt service and improves his overall cash flow.

Assuming a 3 percent annual appreciation rate, the value of his portfolio increases to approximately $14,000,000 by year five. At the same time, his loan balances decrease, resulting in substantial equity growth. If his total loan balance is approximately $10,000,000, he has built $4,000,000 in equity. This example demonstrates how a consistent pipeline can transform your strategy. Instead of relying on a single deal, Carlos creates a system that generates opportunities and converts them into growth. By focusing on process and consistency, he is able to build a significant portfolio in a relatively short period of time.

The key takeaway is that success with SBA 504 loans is not just about individual transactions—it is about building a system that produces results over time. By creating and managing a strong acquisition pipeline, you can achieve predictable growth and long-term financial success.

Chapter 12

Creating a Complete SBA 504 Wealth System and Your Long-Term Execution Plan

At this point, you have learned how SBA 504 loans work, how to qualify, how to structure deals, optimize cash flow, manage risk, build a pipeline, and scale a portfolio. Now it is time to bring everything together into a complete system—a repeatable, disciplined, and scalable approach that allows you to consistently acquire, manage, and grow commercial real estate using SBA 504 financing. This chapter is about execution. It is about turning knowledge into action and building a long-term system that produces results year after year.

The first step in creating your SBA 504 wealth system is defining your long-term vision. This goes beyond simply owning property. You must decide what you want your portfolio to look like in five, ten, or even twenty years. This includes the number of properties, the types of assets, the level of cash flow you want to generate, and the amount of equity you aim to build. Having a clear vision provides direction and ensures that every decision you make aligns with your goals.

Once your vision is defined, the next step is creating a clear acquisition plan. This involves determining how many properties you want to acquire each year, what price range you are targeting, and how much capital you are willing to invest. For example, you may decide to acquire one property per year with an average purchase price of $2,500,000. With a 10 percent down payment, this would require $250,000 per year in capital. By breaking your goals into manageable steps, you create a roadmap that makes your vision achievable.

Consistency is the foundation of this system. Rather than waiting for the perfect deal, you focus on executing your plan consistently over time. This means maintaining your pipeline, analyzing opportunities, and making decisions based on your criteria. Some years you may acquire more properties, and other years fewer, but the key is to stay active and engaged in the process.

Financial discipline is another critical component. As your portfolio grows, so does your responsibility to manage it effectively. This includes maintaining accurate financial records, monitoring cash flow, and ensuring that each property performs as expected. It also means avoiding unnecessary risk, such as overleveraging or taking on deals that do not meet your criteria. Reinvestment is a key driver of long-term growth. As your properties generate cash flow and appreciate in value, you can reinvest those gains into new opportunities. This creates a compounding effect, where each successful investment contributes to the next. Over time, this cycle can significantly accelerate your growth and help you achieve your financial goals more quickly.

Another important element of your system is adaptability. Markets change, interest rates fluctuate, and new opportunities emerge. While your long-term vision should remain consistent, your strategy may need to evolve. Being flexible and open to adjusting your approach allows you to take advantage of new opportunities while minimizing risk.

Building a strong team is essential for executing your system effectively. This includes lenders, CDCs, real estate agents, attorneys, accountants, and property managers who understand your strategy and can support your growth. As your portfolio expands, having the right team in place allows you to operate more efficiently and focus on high-level decision-making.

Time management is also critical. As you balance your business operations with your real estate investments, it is important to allocate your time effectively. This may involve setting aside specific times for deal analysis, networking, and property management. Over time, you may also delegate certain tasks to your team, allowing you to focus on strategy and growth.

Another key component of your SBA 504 wealth system is performance tracking. This involves regularly reviewing your portfolio to assess how each property is performing. Key metrics may include cash flow, occupancy rates, property value, and return on investment. By tracking these metrics, you can identify areas for improvement and make informed decisions about future investments.

Long-term risk management remains an ongoing priority. As your portfolio grows, so does your exposure to potential risks. Maintaining reserves, diversifying your properties, and staying informed about market conditions helps protect your investments and ensure long-term stability.

Your exit strategy should also be integrated into your system. Whether you plan to hold properties for long-term cash flow, refinance to access equity, or sell at a profit, having a clear exit plan allows you to make strategic decisions throughout the life of each investment. This ensures that you are always moving toward your long-term goals.

One of the most powerful aspects of building an SBA 504 wealth system is the shift in mindset. You move from thinking about individual deals to thinking about systems, processes, and long-term outcomes. This shift allows you to operate more strategically and make decisions that support sustained growth.

Over time, as your system becomes more refined, you will begin to see predictable results. Your pipeline will consistently generate opportunities, your deals will become more efficient, and your portfolio will grow steadily. This predictability is what transforms real estate investing from a series of isolated transactions into a scalable business.

Ultimately, creating a complete SBA 504 wealth system is about taking control of your financial future. It is about building a structure that supports your goals, allows you to grow consistently, and provides long-term security and independence. By applying the principles in this chapter, you can turn your knowledge into action and create a system that delivers results for years to come.

Real-Life Math Example: Building a 10-Year SBA 504 Wealth System

Let's walk through a comprehensive example to illustrate how a complete SBA 504 system can produce significant financial results over time. In this scenario, we will follow a borrower named Elena, who owns a professional services business and commits to acquiring one property per year for 10 years.

Elena sets a goal of purchasing properties with an average price of $2,500,000. Each year, she invests 10 percent, or $250,000, as her down payment. Over 10 years, her total investment is $2,500,000.

Each property generates an average of $5,000 per month in rental income, or $60,000 per year. By year ten, Elena owns 10 properties generating a combined rental income of $50,000 per month, or $600,000 per year.

Now let's examine the appreciation. Assuming a 3 percent annual increase in property value, each property purchased in year one grows to approximately $3,360,000 by year ten. Properties purchased in later years appreciate accordingly based on their timeline. The total portfolio value after 10 years is approximately $30,000,000.

At the same time, Elena's loan balances decrease due to amortization. If her total remaining loan balance across all properties is approximately $22,000,000, she has built $8,000,000 in equity.

In addition to equity growth, Elena benefits from rental income and reduced occupancy costs for her business. Over 10 years, her properties generate millions in rental income, which she reinvests into her business and additional investments.

Now let's calculate her return on investment. Elena invested $2,500,000 over 10 years. She now has $8,000,000 in equity, plus significant cash flow. This represents a substantial return and demonstrates the power of consistency and compounding.

This example highlights how building a system, rather than focusing on individual deals, can lead to predictable and scalable growth. By following a disciplined approach, Elena is able to transform her initial investment into a multi-million-dollar portfolio.

The key takeaway is that success with SBA 504 loans is not about a single transaction—it is about building a system that produces results over time. By committing to your plan, maintaining discipline, and continuously improving your approach, you can create a powerful wealth-building engine that supports your long-term goals.

Chapter 13

Advanced Tax Strategies, Wealth Preservation, and Legacy Planning with SBA 504 Real Estate

As your SBA 504 portfolio grows, your focus naturally shifts from acquisition and scaling to preservation, optimization, and long-term legacy. At this stage, the goal is no longer just to build wealth—it is to protect it, multiply it efficiently, and transfer it in a way that benefits future generations. This chapter explores advanced strategies that high-level investors and business owners use to maximize after-tax returns, preserve capital, and create a lasting financial legacy through SBA 504-financed real estate.

One of the most powerful advantages of owning commercial real estate is the ability to leverage tax-efficient strategies. While this book does not replace professional tax advice, understanding the general principles allows you to work more effectively with your accountant and make more strategic decisions. The key idea is that real estate offers unique opportunities to reduce taxable income while increasing actual cash flow, creating a gap between what you earn and what you are taxed on. Depreciation is one of the most significant tools in this strategy. When you own commercial real estate, you can depreciate the value of the building over time, even if the property is increasing in market value. This creates a non-cash expense that reduces your taxable income. For example, if your property generates $200,000 in annual net income but you claim $100,000 in depreciation, you may only be taxed on $100,000, even though your actual cash flow is higher. This allows you to retain more of your earnings and reinvest them into your business or additional properties.

Cost segregation is a more advanced version of this concept. By breaking down the components of a property into different categories with shorter depreciation schedules, you can accelerate your depreciation deductions. This can significantly reduce your taxable income in the early years of ownership, improving your cash flow and providing additional capital for reinvestment. While this strategy requires professional analysis, it is widely used by experienced investors to enhance returns.

Interest deductions are another important benefit. The interest portion of your SBA 504 loan payments is typically deductible, further reducing your taxable income. Combined with depreciation, this can create a powerful tax shield that allows you to keep more of your earnings. This is one of the reasons why real estate is often considered one of the most tax-efficient asset classes.

Another key strategy for wealth preservation is entity structuring. As your portfolio grows, it becomes increasingly important to separate your assets into different legal entities. This can provide liability protection, simplify management, and create flexibility for future transactions. For example, you may hold each property in a separate entity while operating your business in another. This structure helps protect your assets and ensures that issues with one property do not impact others.

Asset protection is closely tied to this concept. Protecting your wealth from potential risks such as lawsuits, economic downturns, or operational challenges is essential for long-term success. This includes maintaining adequate insurance coverage, structuring your entities properly, and working with legal professionals who understand your strategy. The goal is to create layers of protection that safeguard your assets while allowing you to continue growing your portfolio.

As your wealth increases, estate and legacy planning become more important. This involves determining how your assets will be transferred to future generations and ensuring that your wealth is preserved over time. Without proper planning, a significant portion of your estate could be lost to taxes or mismanagement. By creating a clear plan, you can ensure that your assets are transferred efficiently and aligned with your intentions.

One common strategy is to gradually transfer ownership of your properties to family members or trusts. This can help reduce estate taxes and ensure a smooth transition of assets. Trusts can also provide additional benefits, such as asset protection and control over how your wealth is distributed. While these strategies require professional guidance, understanding their purpose allows you to make more informed decisions.

Another important aspect of legacy planning is education. Passing on wealth without passing on knowledge can lead to poor decision-making and loss of assets. By educating your family about your investments, strategies, and values, you create a foundation for long-term success. This ensures that your wealth continues to grow and benefit future generations.

Cash flow management remains critical even at this advanced stage. While your focus may shift toward preservation, maintaining strong cash flow ensures that your portfolio remains sustainable. This includes managing expenses, optimizing rental income, and reinvesting profits strategically. A well-managed portfolio not only generates income but also provides flexibility for future opportunities. Another advanced concept is portfolio diversification. While SBA 504 loans are primarily used for owner-occupied properties, your overall portfolio may include different types of assets, locations, and industries. Diversification reduces risk and increases stability, ensuring that your wealth is not overly dependent on a single asset or market.

Strategic refinancing and capital access also play a role in long-term planning. As your properties appreciate and your equity grows, you may have opportunities to access capital without selling your assets. This allows you to continue investing and expanding while maintaining ownership. However, these decisions should be made carefully, with a focus on long-term stability rather than short-term gains.

Philanthropy is another aspect of legacy planning that many investors consider. As your wealth grows, you may choose to give back to your community or support causes that align with your values. This can be done through charitable donations, foundations, or other structures that provide both personal fulfillment and potential tax benefits.

Ultimately, advanced tax strategies, wealth preservation, and legacy planning are about creating a system that not only builds wealth but also sustains it over time. It is about making decisions that protect your assets, optimize your returns, and ensure that your efforts benefit not only you but also future generations.

By integrating these strategies into your SBA 504 approach, you move beyond simple investing and into long-term wealth stewardship. You create a structure that supports growth, protects against risk, and provides lasting value. This is the final stage of mastery—where your investments become not just a source of income, but a foundation for generational wealth.

Real-Life Math Example: Tax Efficiency, Wealth Preservation, and Long-Term Legacy Growth

Let's walk through a detailed example to illustrate how advanced strategies can enhance long-term wealth using SBA 504-financed properties. In this scenario, we will follow a borrower named Victor, who has built a portfolio of five commercial properties over several years.

Victor's portfolio has a total value of $15,000,000 and generates $900,000 in annual net operating income. His total loan balance is $10,000,000, and his annual debt service is $600,000, leaving him with $300,000 in pre-tax cash flow.

Now let's examine the impact of depreciation. Suppose Victor's properties allow him to claim $400,000 in annual depreciation. This reduces his taxable income from $300,000 to negative $100,000. While he still generates $300,000 in actual cash flow, his taxable income is significantly reduced, allowing him to retain more of his earnings.

Next, we consider interest deductions. If $250,000 of his annual debt service is interest, this further reduces his taxable income. Combined with depreciation, Victor's tax liability is minimized, improving his overall financial position.

Now let's look at long-term appreciation. Assuming a 3 percent annual increase in property value, Victor's portfolio grows from $15,000,000 to approximately $20,160,000 over 10 years. During the same period, his loan balance decreases to around $7,000,000, resulting in $13,160,000 in equity.

Victor also continues to generate cash flow during this time. Over 10 years, his $300,000 annual cash flow totals $3,000,000, much of which is reinvested into additional opportunities.

Now let's consider legacy planning. Victor transfers ownership of his properties into a trust structure designed to benefit his children. This allows him to reduce potential estate taxes and ensure that his assets are managed according to his wishes.

By combining tax efficiency, appreciation, cash flow, and

strategic planning, Victor transforms his portfolio into a long-term wealth engine. His initial investments grow into a multi-million-dollar estate that provides income, stability, and opportunities for future generations.

This example demonstrates how advanced strategies can significantly enhance the benefits of SBA 504 financing. By focusing on both growth and preservation, you can create a financial system that not only builds wealth but also sustains it for years to come.

Chapter 14

Turning SBA 504 Expertise into a Business Model and Creating Multiple Income Streams

By now, you've mastered how to use SBA 504 loans to acquire, optimize, and scale commercial real estate. But there is another level—one that very few people reach. That level is turning your knowledge, experience, and deal flow into a business model itself. Instead of only making money from owning real estate, you begin generating income from structuring deals, creating partnerships, consulting, and building systems that produce revenue in multiple ways. This is where SBA 504 expertise evolves into a true financial engine.

The first shift you must make is seeing yourself not just as a borrower or investor, but as a deal architect. Once you understand how SBA 504 loans work, how to structure them, and how to get them approved, you possess a skill that is extremely valuable in the marketplace. Most business owners do not understand SBA financing at this level, which creates an opportunity for you to step in and guide them. This guidance can become a service, a partnership opportunity, or even a full-scale business. One of the simplest ways to create additional income is by consulting or advising other business owners. Many entrepreneurs want to buy their own building but do not know where to start. By helping them understand the process, structure their deal, and connect with the right lenders and CDCs, you can provide significant value. This can be structured as a consulting fee, a success fee, or even a percentage of the deal. Over time, as your reputation grows, this can become a consistent and scalable income stream.

Another powerful strategy is forming joint ventures. Instead of simply advising, you can partner with business owners who want to acquire property but lack the experience or confidence. In these arrangements, you bring your expertise and potentially some capital, while they bring the business and operational side. Together, you structure and execute the deal. In return, you may receive equity in the property, a share of the cash flow, or both. This allows you to participate in deals without being the sole investor.

Deal sourcing itself can also become a business. As you build your pipeline and network, you will come across opportunities that you may not want to pursue personally. Instead of letting these deals go to waste, you can assign them, partner on them, or connect them with other buyers. This creates another layer of value, as you are effectively monetizing your ability to find and identify opportunities. Another advanced strategy is creating systems and platforms around your expertise. For example, you can build a network of lenders, CDCs, brokers, and business owners, positioning yourself at the center of these relationships. By facilitating connections and helping deals come together, you become a key player in the ecosystem. This can lead to referral income, partnership opportunities, and long-term relationships that generate ongoing revenue.

Education is another powerful income stream. As you've experienced throughout this series, there is significant demand for clear, actionable knowledge about SBA 504 loans and commercial real estate. By creating courses, books, or training programs, you can share your expertise with a broader audience. This not only generates income but also enhances your credibility and expands your network.

You can also integrate SBA 504 financing into your existing business. For example, if you are in real estate, lending, or consulting, offering SBA 504 expertise as part of your services can differentiate you from competitors and attract more clients. This creates a synergy between your existing operations and your real estate strategy, increasing your overall profitability.

Another opportunity lies in building a brand around your expertise. By positioning yourself as a specialist in SBA 504 financing, you attract opportunities, partnerships, and clients. This can be done through content creation, networking, and consistent communication of your value. Over time, your brand becomes a magnet for deals and opportunities.

Scaling these income streams requires systems and delegation. As your activities expand, you cannot do everything yourself. Building a team or leveraging technology allows you to handle more deals, clients, and opportunities without becoming overwhelmed. This includes systems for lead generation, deal analysis, communication, and follow-up.

One of the most important aspects of turning your expertise into a business is maintaining integrity and alignment. The goal is not just to generate income, but to create value for others. By focusing on helping others succeed, you build trust and long-term relationships, which ultimately lead to more opportunities and sustainable growth.

Risk management also applies at this level. As you engage in partnerships, consulting, and deal structuring, it is important to clearly define roles, responsibilities, and expectations. Proper agreements and professional guidance ensure that your interests are protected and that all parties are aligned.

As you build multiple income streams, you create financial diversification. Instead of relying solely on rental income or appreciation, you generate revenue from various sources. This reduces risk and increases stability, allowing you to weather market changes and continue growing.

The ultimate goal is to create a system where your knowledge, network, and experience work together to generate consistent opportunities and income. You move from being a participant in the market to being a creator of opportunities. This shift not only increases your income potential but also gives you greater control over your financial future.

By turning your SBA 504 expertise into a business model, you unlock a new level of potential. You are no longer limited by your own capital or the number of properties you can personally acquire. Instead, you leverage your knowledge to participate in multiple deals, create multiple income streams, and build a scalable financial ecosystem.

Real-Life Math Example: Creating Multiple Income Streams from SBA 504 Expertise

Let's walk through a detailed example to illustrate how SBA 504 expertise can be transformed into multiple income streams. In this scenario, we will follow a borrower named Marcus, who has successfully completed several SBA 504 deals and decides to expand his strategy beyond property ownership.

Marcus currently owns three properties valued at a total of $9,000,000. These properties generate $25,000 per month in rental income, or $300,000 per year. After expenses and debt service, his net cash flow is approximately $120,000 per year.

Now, Marcus begins offering consulting services to other business owners. He helps five clients per year structure SBA 504 deals, charging a $10,000 fee per client. This generates an additional $50,000 per year in income.

Next, Marcus forms joint ventures on two deals per year. Each deal is valued at $3,000,000, and Marcus negotiates a 10 percent equity stake in each property. Over time, as these properties appreciate and generate income, his equity grows significantly. For simplicity, assume each deal generates $15,000 per year in cash flow for Marcus, resulting in $30,000 annually.

Marcus also monetizes his deal pipeline by sourcing opportunities and partnering with other investors. He participates in three additional deals per year, earning $15,000 per deal through partnerships or referral structures. This adds another $45,000 per year.

Finally, Marcus creates an online course teaching SBA 504 strategies. He sells the course for $500 and attracts 200 students per year, generating $100,000 in revenue.

Now let's total his income streams:

- Rental income (net): $120,000
- Consulting: $50,000
- Joint ventures: $30,000
- Deal sourcing: $45,000
- Course sales: $100,000

Total annual income: $345,000

This is nearly three times the income Marcus was generating from real estate alone. Additionally, his equity continues to grow as his properties appreciate. Assuming a 3 percent annual appreciation rate, his $9,000,000 portfolio grows to approximately $12,093,000 over 10 years.

At the same time, his joint venture equity and additional investments further increase his net worth. Combined with his multiple income streams, Marcus has created a highly diversified and scalable financial system.

This example demonstrates how SBA 504 expertise can be leveraged far beyond individual property ownership. By creating multiple income streams, Marcus not only increases his earnings but also reduces risk and builds a more resilient financial future. The key takeaway is that your knowledge is an asset. When combined with action, systems, and strategy, it becomes a powerful tool for creating opportunities, generating income, and building long-term wealth.

Chapter 15

The Complete SBA 504 Mastery Blueprint — From First Deal to Financial Freedom

Reaching this point in the journey means you now possess something extremely powerful: a complete understanding of how SBA 504 mortgage loans can be used not just to acquire property, but to build a scalable, strategic, and long-term wealth system. This final chapter is about putting everything together into a clear, repeatable blueprint that takes you from your first deal all the way to financial freedom. It is about simplifying complexity, creating clarity, and giving you a step-by-step path that you can follow regardless of where you are starting.

The first phase of the blueprint is preparation. Before you ever look at a property, you must position yourself as a strong borrower. This includes organizing your financials, improving your credit profile, understanding your business cash flow, and building relationships with lenders and CDCs. Preparation is what allows you to move quickly and confidently when opportunities arise. Without it, even the best deal can slip through your hands. The second phase is deal identification.

This is where your pipeline becomes critical. You must consistently generate opportunities through brokers, direct outreach, and your network. The goal is not to find one perfect deal, but to create a steady flow of potential deals so you can choose the best ones. This phase is about activity, consistency, and positioning yourself in the market.

The third phase is deal analysis. Every opportunity must be evaluated against your criteria. This includes purchase price, cash flow potential, location, property condition, and alignment with SBA 504 requirements. You must be disciplined in your analysis, avoiding emotional decisions and focusing on data. A strong deal is one that not only works today but continues to perform over time.

The fourth phase is structuring the deal. This is where you apply everything you have learned about SBA 504 loans. You determine the optimal loan structure, down payment, and use of the property. You look for ways to maximize cash flow, such as leasing unused space or including improvements in the project cost. This phase is about turning a good deal into a great one.

The fifth phase is execution. This involves navigating the loan process, managing documentation, coordinating with lenders and CDCs, and moving the deal to closing. Execution requires organization, communication, and persistence. It is where many deals are lost due to delays or lack of follow-through. Mastering this phase ensures that your efforts result in successful acquisitions.

The sixth phase is optimization. Once the property is acquired, your focus shifts to maximizing its performance. This includes increasing rental income, controlling expenses, improving operations, and enhancing the property's value. Optimization is what transforms a property from an asset into a high-performing investment.

The seventh phase is scaling. With one successful deal completed, you repeat the process. You use your experience, equity, and cash flow to pursue additional opportunities. Over time, this creates a portfolio of properties that generate income and build equity. Scaling is where the compounding effect begins to take hold.

The eighth phase is diversification. As your portfolio grows, you expand into different property types, locations, and income streams. This reduces risk and increases stability. It also allows you to take advantage of different market opportunities and build a more resilient portfolio.

The ninth phase is preservation. At this stage, your focus shifts toward protecting your wealth. This includes managing risk, optimizing taxes, and structuring your assets for long-term stability. Preservation ensures that the wealth you have built is not lost due to poor planning or unforeseen events.

The tenth and final phase is legacy. This is where your efforts extend beyond your own financial goals and into creating lasting impact. Whether it is providing for your family, supporting your community, or building a business that continues beyond you, this phase is about ensuring that your work has long-term significance.

Throughout this blueprint, one principle remains constant: consistency. Success with SBA 504 loans is not about a single deal or a single decision. It is about executing this process repeatedly over time. Each deal builds on the previous one, creating momentum and accelerating your growth.

Another important principle is leverage. By using SBA 504 loans, you are able to control large assets with relatively small amounts of capital. This amplifies your returns and allows you to scale more quickly. However, leverage must be used responsibly, with careful attention to cash flow and risk management.

Mindset also plays a critical role. Building a portfolio of commercial real estate requires patience, discipline, and long-term thinking. There will be challenges, delays, and setbacks, but maintaining focus on your goals allows you to navigate these obstacles and continue moving forward.

As you implement this blueprint, you will begin to see patterns in your success. You will become more efficient in identifying deals, more confident in structuring them, and more effective in managing your properties. This progression is what transforms you from a beginner into an expert.

The ultimate goal of this blueprint is financial freedom. This does not necessarily mean stopping work, but rather having the flexibility to choose how you spend your time. With a portfolio that generates consistent cash flow and builds equity, you gain control over your financial future.

This blueprint is not theoretical—it is practical and actionable. It is designed to be followed, refined, and adapted to your specific situation. By committing to this process and executing it consistently, you can achieve results that go far beyond what most people believe is possible.

This is the culmination of the SBA Commercial Mortgage Loan Mastery Series. You now have the knowledge, the strategy, and the framework to take action. The next step is yours.

Real-Life Math Example: From First Deal to Financial Freedom Using the SBA 504 Blueprint

Let's walk through a complete example to illustrate how this blueprint can lead to financial freedom. In this scenario, we will follow a borrower named Daniel, who starts with limited capital but commits to executing the SBA 504 strategy over a 12-year period.

In year one, Daniel purchases his first property for $2,000,000 using an SBA 504 loan. He invests $200,000 as a down payment. The property generates $3,000 per month in rental income, reducing his effective cost and improving his cash flow.

Over the next three years, Daniel focuses on optimization. He increases rental income to $5,000 per month and improves his business operations. The property appreciates to approximately $2,250,000, and his loan balance decreases, giving him $400,000 in equity.

In year four, Daniel acquires a second property for $2,800,000 with a $280,000 down payment. This property generates $7,000 per month in rental income. His combined portfolio now produces $12,000 per month in rental income.

By year six, Daniel owns two properties valued at approximately $5,500,000. His equity has grown to over $1,200,000, and his rental income continues to increase.

In year seven, Daniel acquires a third property for $3,500,000 with a $350,000 down payment. This property generates $10,000 per month in rental income. His total rental income now reaches $22,000 per month.

By year ten, Daniel owns three properties valued at approximately $8,500,000. His equity exceeds $3,000,000, and his rental income reaches $25,000 per month.

In year twelve, Daniel acquires a fourth property for $4,000,000 with a $400,000 down payment. This property generates $12,000 per month in rental income. His total rental income now exceeds $37,000 per month, or $444,000 per year.

Let's analyze the results. Daniel's total investment over 12 years is approximately $1,230,000. His portfolio is now worth over $12,500,000, with equity exceeding $5,000,000. His rental income provides a strong and consistent cash flow that supports his lifestyle and future investments.

At this stage, Daniel has achieved financial freedom. His income from real estate exceeds his living expenses, and his portfolio continues to grow through appreciation and amortization. He now has the flexibility to reinvest, expand, or focus on other opportunities. This example demonstrates the power of the SBA 504 blueprint. By starting with one deal and consistently executing the process, Daniel transforms a relatively small initial investment into a multi-million-dollar portfolio and a reliable income stream.

The key takeaway is that financial freedom is not achieved overnight. It is built step by step, deal by deal, through consistent action and disciplined execution. By following this blueprint, you can create a system that produces long-term results and allows you to take control of your financial future.

Closing Thoughts

Your Next Move Defines Your Future

As you reach the end of *The SBA Commercial Mortgage Loan Mastery Series*, it is important to recognize that this is not the end of your journey—it is the beginning of a new level of execution. Knowledge alone does not create results. Strategy alone does not create wealth. The combination of knowledge, strategy, and consistent action is what transforms your financial future. What you choose to do after this moment will ultimately determine the results you achieve.

Throughout this series, you have learned how to think differently about commercial real estate. You have moved beyond the traditional mindset of saving money slowly or relying solely on income from a job or business. Instead, you now understand how to use leverage, structure, and strategic financing to accelerate your growth. You have learned how SBA 504 loans can be used not just to acquire property, but to build a system that produces income, equity, and long-term financial stability.

The most important realization is that these opportunities are not reserved for large corporations or institutional investors. They are available to individuals who are willing to learn, plan, and take action. The difference between those who succeed and those who do not is rarely intelligence or access—it is execution. It is the willingness to move forward, even when the process feels complex or uncertain.

There will always be reasons to wait. The market may not feel perfect. Interest rates may seem too high or too low. You may feel like you need more experience, more capital, or more time. But the reality is that there will never be a perfect moment. The individuals who build wealth are those who act despite uncertainty, who learn through experience, and who refine their approach over time.

Your first deal is not about perfection—it is about progress. It is about stepping into the process, applying what you have learned, and gaining real-world experience. That first deal creates momentum. It builds confidence. It opens doors to new opportunities. And most importantly, it transforms your mindset from someone who is learning into someone who is doing.

As you move forward, remember that consistency is your greatest advantage. You do not need to complete ten deals in one year to succeed. What matters is that you continue moving forward, deal by deal, year by year. Over time, this consistency creates compounding results that far exceed what most people expect. You will encounter challenges along the way. There will be deals that do not work out, properties that require more effort than expected, and moments where progress feels slow. These challenges are not failures—they are part of the process. Each one provides valuable lessons that strengthen your ability to make better decisions in the future.

Building wealth through SBA 504 loans is not a short-term strategy. It is a long-term commitment to growth, discipline, and strategic thinking. It requires patience, but it also offers stability and predictability that few other investment strategies can match. Over time, as your properties appreciate, your loans are paid down, and your income increases, you will begin to see the true power of this approach.

Another important concept to carry forward is control. Owning your commercial property gives you control over your environment, your expenses, and your future. You are no longer subject to the decisions of landlords or market fluctuations in rent. Instead, you are building equity in assets that you own and control. This shift in control is one of the most empowering aspects of this strategy.

As your portfolio grows, your perspective will change. You will begin to see opportunities that others overlook. You will recognize patterns in the market. You will develop the confidence to make decisions that align with your long-term goals. This evolution is what transforms you from a participant in the market into a strategist who creates opportunities.

Financial freedom, as discussed throughout this series, is not just about money. It is about options. It is about having the ability to choose how you spend your time, where you focus your energy, and what kind of life you want to create. It is about reducing stress, increasing security, and building a future that aligns with your values.

For some, financial freedom may mean stepping away from daily operations and focusing on personal interests. For others, it may mean continuing to build and expand, driven by the excitement of growth and opportunity. There is no single definition—the key is that you have the freedom to choose.

As you think about your future, consider not only what you want to achieve, but also who you want to become. The process of building a portfolio, managing investments, and executing deals will shape your mindset, your habits, and your approach to challenges. This growth is just as valuable as the financial results.

Another important aspect to consider is impact. As you build your portfolio and expand your capabilities, you create opportunities not only for yourself but also for others. This may include providing space for businesses to grow, creating jobs, or sharing your knowledge with others who are starting their own journey. Your success has the potential to extend far beyond your personal goals.

Legacy is the final layer of this journey. The assets you build, the systems you create, and the knowledge you acquire can be passed on to future generations. This is how wealth becomes more than just numbers—it becomes a foundation for long-term stability and opportunity. By thinking beyond your immediate goals, you create something that endures.

At this point, you have everything you need to begin. You have the knowledge, the framework, and the strategies. What remains is action. Start where you are. Use what you have. Take the first step. Then take the next one.

Each decision you make from this point forward contributes to your trajectory. Each deal, each relationship, each lesson builds on the last. Over time, these small steps compound into significant results.

The SBA 504 loan is not just a financing tool—it is a pathway. A pathway to ownership, to growth, to stability, and ultimately to freedom. It is a system that, when used correctly, can transform your financial life.

Now the question is simple: what will you do next?

Will you wait for the perfect moment, or will you take action today?

Will you remain where you are, or will you step into the opportunity in front of you?

The choice is yours. And with that choice comes the potential to create something extraordinary.

This is your starting point.

How to Get a Personalized SBA Commercial Mortgage Review

If you found this book helpful, you may want to see how these strategies apply to your specific financial situation.

SBA commercial mortgage financing is highly customized—your business income, financial statements, credit profile, property type, industry, and long-term goals all play a role in determining what you qualify for and how your loan should be structured.

Every borrower's situation is different. Your revenue trends, business model, tax returns, debt obligations, ownership structure, and the type of commercial property you are purchasing, refinancing, or building all impact your options. The strategies and examples in this book are designed to teach you how SBA commercial mortgage loans work—but your actual loan approval, terms, and structure can only be determined by analyzing your real financial profile.

If you would like a no-obligation SBA Commercial Mortgage review, you can request one here:

Email: info@FinibiMortgage.com

A licensed mortgage broker will review your business financials, income structure, credit profile, and goals, and explain what SBA financing options may be available to you—including:

• SBA 7(a) commercial mortgage loans• SBA 504 fixed-rate commercial real estate financing• Owner-occupied property qualification strategies• Business acquisition with real estate financing• Commercial refinance and cash-out strategies• Construction and expansion loan structuring• Advanced SBA deal structuring to maximize approval

No cost. No pressure. No obligation.

Sincerely,

Joseph G. Correa

Finibi Mortgage Inc.

Licensed Mortgage Broker

About the Author

Joseph G. Correa is a licensed mortgage broker and the founder of Finibi Mortgage, a Florida-based brokerage specializing in SBA commercial mortgage loans, non-QM lending, and strategic real estate financing solutions for business owners, entrepreneurs, and investors.

With more than two decades of experience in mortgage lending, underwriting, and deal structuring, Joseph has helped thousands of clients secure financing for commercial real estate, business acquisitions, and complex transactions using both traditional and alternative lending strategies.

Unlike traditional loan officers who focus only on basic qualification, Joseph's approach emphasizes **cash flow analysis, deal structuring, and strategic financing**. He believes that business owners should not be limited by rigid lending formulas, but instead empowered by understanding how to structure deals that align with lender guidelines and maximize approval potential.

Joseph is widely recognized for his expertise in:

• SBA 7(a) and SBA 504 commercial mortgage loans• Owner-occupied commercial real estate financing• Business acquisition with real estate structuring• Commercial refinance and cash flow optimization• Construction and expansion financing• Advanced loan structuring and approval strategy

Through his education platform, Finibi Academy, Joseph has trained tens of thousands of students worldwide in mortgage strategy, real estate investing, credit optimization, and financial independence.

He created the *SBA Commercial Mortgage Loan Mastery Series* to provide a clear, step-by-step roadmap for borrowers and professionals who want to understand, qualify for, and scale commercial real estate using SBA financing.

His mission is simple:

To help business owners use strategic financing to acquire assets, build cash flow, and create long-term wealth.

When he is not structuring loans or writing, Joseph works with clients across the United States to design customized SBA financing strategies aligned with their business goals and growth plans.

The SBA Commercial Mortgage Loan Mastery Series Roadmap

The Complete Guide to Using SBA Financing to Build Commercial Real Estate and Business Wealth

The purpose of *The SBA Commercial Mortgage Loan Mastery Series* is to give business owners, investors, and mortgage professionals the exact strategies used by lenders and underwriters—translated into simple, practical steps you can apply in real life.

This series takes you from beginner to advanced mastery of how to qualify, structure, and scale commercial real estate and business financing using SBA mortgage loans.

Each book builds on the last. You are not just learning how to get approved—you are learning how to control your approvals and scale your opportunities.

Book 1 — SBA Commercial Mortgage Loan Fundamentals Understand how SBA mortgage programs work, including 7(a) and 504 loans, and how to qualify.

Book 2 — Getting Approved for an SBA Commercial Mortgage Loan Learn step-by-step strategies to meet lender requirements and secure funding.

Book 3 — Owner-Occupied Property Financing with SBA Loans Learn how to buy or refinance your business property using SBA financing.

Book 4 — Buying a Business and Real Estate with SBA Financing Acquire a business and its property in one structured transaction.

Book 5 — SBA 7(a) Mortgage Loan Strategies Master flexible loan structures for business and real estate funding.

Book 6 — SBA 504 Mortgage Loans for Commercial Real Estate Use long-term fixed-rate financing for large property acquisitions.

Book 7 — Refinancing Commercial Debt with SBA Loans Lower payments, improve cash flow, and restructure existing debt.

Book 8 — SBA Loans for Construction and Expansion Build, renovate, and scale commercial properties with structured financing.

Book 9 — SBA Loan Requirements, Rates, and Structures Understand how to compare options and choose the best loan.

Book 10 — Advanced SBA Commercial Mortgage Structuring Engineer approvals and maximize leverage using expert strategies.

This series is designed to move you from:

Understanding → Execution → Scaling → Mastery

By the end, you will not just know how to qualify—you will know how to structure, analyze, and scale deals like a professional.

Educational & Financial Disclaimer

The *SBA Commercial Mortgage Loan Mastery Series* is intended for educational and informational purposes only.

This content is designed to help readers understand SBA commercial mortgage lending, real estate financing strategies, and business acquisition concepts. It is not financial, legal, tax, or investment advice.

Joseph G. Correa and Live Stronger Faster are not acting as your personal financial advisor, attorney, accountant, or mortgage professional through this publication.

SBA loan programs, underwriting guidelines, interest rates, and lender requirements may change at any time and vary by lender.

All examples in this series are for illustration purposes only and do not guarantee approval or results.

Always consult with licensed professionals before making financial decisions.

Risk Disclosure

SBA commercial mortgage lending and real estate investing involve risk.

Business performance, income stability, interest rate changes, market conditions, and lender guidelines can all impact loan approval and financial outcomes.

Borrowing against real estate or using leverage increases both potential returns and risk.

Failure to repay a loan may result in foreclosure and loss of property.

Cash flow, rental income, appreciation, and business performance are not guaranteed.

All strategies presented in this series are educational and must be evaluated based on your individual financial situation.

You are solely responsible for your financial decisions.

www.ingramcontent.com/pod-product-compliance
Ingram Content Group UK Ltd.
Pitfield, Milton Keynes, MK11 3LW, UK
UKHW020158290926
15471UKWH00005B/949

9 798295 820601